ISBN 978-1-332-43467-1
PIBN 10025242

English
Français
Deutsche
Italiano
Español
Português

www.forgottenbooks.com

Mythology Photography **Fiction**
Fishing Christianity **Art** Cooking
Essays Buddhism Freemasonry
Medicine **Biology** Music **Ancient
Egypt** Evolution Carpentry Physics
Dance Geology **Mathematics** Fitness
Shakespeare **Folklore** Yoga Marketing
Confidence Immortality Biographies
Poetry **Psychology** Witchcraft
Electronics Chemistry History **Law**
Accounting **Philosophy** Anthropology
Alchemy Drama Quantum Mechanics
Atheism Sexual Health **Ancient History**
Entrepreneurship Languages Sport
Paleontology Needlework Islam
Metaphysics Investment Archaeology
Parenting Statistics Criminology
Motivational

BULLETIN OF THE UNIVERSITY OF WISCONSIN

NO. 247

ECONOMICS AND POLITICAL SCIENCE SERIES, VOL. 5, No. 1, PP. 1-178

THE FINANCIAL HISTORY OF KANSAS

BY

JAMES ERNEST BOYLE

Professor of Economics and Political Science
University of North Dakota

A THESIS SUBMITTED FOR THE DEGREE OF DOCTOR OF PHILOSOPHY

UNIVERSITY OF WISCONSIN

1904

Published bi-monthly by authority of law with the approval of the Regents
of the University and entered as second-class matter
at the post office at Madison, Wisconsin

MADISON, WISCONSIN

AUGUST, 1908

PRICE 50 CENTS

BULLETIN OF THE UNIVERSITY OF WISCONSIN

BULLETIN

OF THE

UNIVERSITY OF WISCONSIN

ECONOMICS AND POLITICAL SCIENCE SERIES

VOLUME V
1908

PUBLISHED BY AUTHORITY OF LAW AND WITH THE APPROVAL OF
THE REGENTS OF THE UNIVERSITY

MADISON, WISCONSIN
1909

BULLETIN OF THE UNIVERSITY OF WISCONSIN

CONTENTS

196947

BULLETIN OF THE UNIVERSITY OF WISCONSIN

NO. 247

ECONOMICS AND POLITICAL SCIENCE SERIES, VOL. 5, No. 1, PP. 1-178

THE FINANCIAL HISTORY OF KANSAS

BY

JAMES ERNEST BOYLE

Professor of Economics and Political Science
University of North Dakota

A THESIS SUBMITTED FOR THE DEGREE OF DOCTOR OF PHILOSOPHY

UNIVERSITY OF WISCONSIN

1904

Published bi-monthly by authority of law with the approval of the Regents
of the University and entered as second-class matter
at the post office at Madison, Wisconsin

MADISON, WISCONSIN
AUGUST, 1908

CONTENTS

[3]

PREFACE

I have used the words "financial history" in a somewhat broad sense. The subject includes, as I have treated it, a consideration of both state and local finances. The word municipality, as used throughout this discussion, applies to any local division of the State, whether a county, township, school district or city. These terms are defined here at the outset, since usage has not yet established uniform meanings for them.

The aim of this work is similar to that of any other standard history, namely, to report and explain facts. It is an attempt, therefore, to trace as faithfully as possible the financial history of the State. Events bearing directly and indirectly on the financial life of the State are narrated and with as little trespassing as possible on the domain of political history. However, financial causes are not divorced from their effects, whether these effects be political, social or economic.

The arrangement of the work is according to the topical and chronological requirements of the subject-matter. An appendix is given at the end, containing valuable statistical data, only part of which appear in the body of the work. A bibliography is also added, showing the sources of information.

Itemized receipts and expenditures have not been tabulated in the usual form, the state system (or rather, lack of system) of accounting rendering such a tabulation useless.

JAMES E. BOYLE.

Madison, Wis., April, 1904.

THE FINANCIAL HISTORY OF KANSAS

CHAPTER I

INTRODUCTORY

The financial history of Kansas has a bearing on practical life which makes it distinctively a live question. This is true for several reasons. A large part of the social income of the State is now used annually to meet the growing expenditures of the State and local divisions. While the resources of the State have increased both in amount and variety, the financial system has maintained that primitive form adapted to a simplicity which no longer exists. This means inevitable injustice, and that for very obvious reasons. For in the early days of the State, land constituted the bulk of the wealth, with a meager showing of personal property. But today, in contrast with this simplicity, we have an almost hopeless complexity, represented by our corporations, manufacturing establishments, mines, transportation companies, municipal franchises, interurban car lines, etc. This complexity in the economic life of the people has increased with sweeping rapidity, while lack of any and all supervising authority in the tax system has caused the doubtful reforms in it to come limping many years behind actual needs. This has augmented certain injustices and developed certain tendencies in the matter of placing the brunt of the burden of taxation on the holders of the simple visible property of the early days of the constitution. And it is a fact too well known to be disputed that the real significance of the burden of taxation is not the size of the burden, but the justice and equity of it. For, as historians have pointed out, our Revolutionary fore-

[9]

fathers rebelled, not at the weight of the taxes on them, which was small, but at their unfairness and injustice. If justice ever existed in Kansas' scheme of taxation, time and change have wrought sad havoc with it, as it is one purpose of this history to show. While there have been no dramatic frauds to mar the financial history of Kansas, and while, in comparison with the financial administrations of great cities like New York, Philadelphia, St. Louis, and Minneapolis, the finances of Kansas have been administered with virtuous honesty, yet the plain, simple question of justice makes the issue not only a live one, but one compelling attention. For the development of wealth along new lines has brought with it an intricate tangle of methods in the taxing system which is hopelessly confusing to the general public. A few initiated ones are in a position to take advantage of this situation, and hence form a privileged class, escaping with mere nominal burdens. And, therefore, it is true that these haphazard methods in the long run give rise to well-intrenched abuses which are more pernicious than the short-lived but more glaring frauds. This breeds discontent and suspicion among the people, as is amply shown by the large number of investigations and impeachments connected with the administration of the public funds. In one year expenditure for these investigations of alleged malfeasance in office ran up to $35,000. There has never been wanting a class, consisting largely of demagogues, who have stood ready to raise the hue and cry of "Fraud;" "Investigate." And hence it is that flagrant frauds have not been perpetrated, but only lesser ones, while the growing evil of injustice has been fastening itself on the fiscal system.

On the whole, then, since the financial system rests on direct taxation, it is a live issue, because taxation has important economic, social and fiscal effects. It modifies the distribution of wealth for the advantage or disadvantage of those concerned; it either promotes the public welfare or works injustice and oppression; and it may embarrass the treasury with too little or too much revenue. These are the facts of taxation today, as common observation will teach, and not its mere potentialities.

Taxable capacity of the State.—A brief survey of the present resources of the State will give a clear understanding of its taxable capacity and will suggest some of its fiscal problems.

Kansas is one of the great agricultural states of the Mississippi valley. The State has an area of 81,700 square miles, or 52,288,000 acres. The population in 1900 was 1,470,495; that is, 18 persons to the square mile, or one person for every 36 acres. At the time of admission into the Union, the Indians held about 10,000,000 acres of land, but their holdings now (1904) are only 105,000 acres. Railroad holdings, once a little over 9,000,000 acres, are now about 1,000,000. There are about 1,000,000 acres, the title to which still vests in the Federal Government. That leaves some 50,000,000 acres of soil, now supposedly used productively in agriculture, grazing and other industries. But in its agricultural conditions, the western part of Kansas differs very much from the eastern. The divergence is marked in the elevation, soil, and rainfall.[1] That portion lying west of the 100th meridian, and some parts extending east of it, belong to the semi-arid or short grass region, where irrigation is necessary for the successful cultivation of most crops. These facts were not known early enough and hence much distress and many failures have occurred in the development of this section. The history of this irrigation in Kansas has been marked by a number of disastrous failures. "Most of them," according to the federal census report,[2] "resulted from a lack of knowledge of the climatic oscillation in the sub-humid regions, and from a fever of speculation in western mortgages. During a cycle of wet years agriculture was extended far into the Plains region. The movement westward was greatly facilitated by companies which were formed to place loans and to take mortgages on real estate, the funds being obtained from the East. As long as the rainfall continued abundant, the profits of these loan agencies were great and the competition became so keen that ordinary prudence was thrown aside. When a series of dry years came, and no crops were made season after season, the land owners abandoned their farms, leaving whole counties practically deserted. The loan companies foreclosed their mortgages and became possessors of large tracts of land which were comparatively valueless.

---

[1] *Census Bulletin.* 12 Census, No. 192, p. 13.
[2] *Census Bulletin.* 12 Census, No. 192, p. 13, 14.

"These ditches and canals have never given adequate returns upon the large investments, owing to the fact that no study had been made of the volume of water in the streams, or of any of the important conditions relating to the diversion of water from them. In order to make their property marketable, the corporations organized new companies, sold stock, and in the southwestern part of the State constructed some of the largest irrigation canals in the United States. The water supply for most of these ditches was taken from the Arkansas river, but after a few years of drought it proved wholly inadequate for the purpose, and hundreds of miles of ditches had to be abandoned. The principal irrigated areas are along this river, where the conditions are somewhat similar to those along the Platte river in Nebraska. Its broad, shallow channel is dry for a considerable part of the year, but water is seeping beneath the surface of the valley lands as well as under the stream bed. The ditches that are operated at the present time can receive water only in times of flood, and are utilized largely in the cultivation of forage crops.

"The reclamation of large areas of fertile and productive land depends upon the adoption and application of successful methods of utilizing the ground waters, which are found throughout western Kansas at varying depths. A partial solution of this problem has been found in the use of windmills and by building small storage reservoirs. The wind, which in the West has heretofore been regarded as an annoyance and a mischief-maker, is harnessed and becomes a factor in promoting progress and development. Irrigation from windmills is no longer an experiment and today many farmers are depending for their living on the products of orchard and garden tracts irrigated by this means. * * * There has been a large increase in the number of irrigators, but not a corresponding increase in the number of acres irrigated. This is explained by the large increase in the number of farms which irrigate small areas by means of windmills and of water pumped from streams, and by a shortage of water for the ditches operated in 1899."

The total area irrigated in 1899 was 23,620 acres, an increase of 13.5 per cent. over 1889.

Kansas has no large cities. Only 22.5 per cent. of her population live in cities of over 2,500 inhabitants, whereas Iowa has 25.6 per cent. urban population, Missouri 36.3, Colorado 48.3, Ohio 48, New York 72.9, and Rhode Island 95. Nebraska has about the same per cent., 23.7.

Agriculture, therefore, has been the predominating industry. Ranking twenty-second in population, the State is seventh in rank in the gross value of agricultural products. These products amounted to $209,895,542 in 1900. Iowa ranked first in the same year with a production worth $365,411,528. The other states outranking Kansas in agricultural products are, after Iowa, Illinois second, Ohio third, New York fourth, Texas fifth and Missouri sixth. The closest rival is Pennsylvania, ranking eighth.

The value of Kansas farm land in 1900, including all improvements, machinery, live stock and other farm property, was $864,100,286, which gave the State the rank of ninth. Illinois ranked first with her valuation of $2,004,316,897; followed by Iowa as second, Ohio third, New York fourth, Pennsylvania fifth, Missouri sixth, Indiana seventh, and Texas eighth. The State ranking tenth, or just below Kansas, was Wisconsin. Second in importance to the agricultural wealth of the State are the railroads. There are seventeen of these roads, and one electric interurban, having in all over 8,800 miles of main track and a total mileage, including side tracks, of over 10,000 miles. Comparing this mileage with the country at large, we find that Kansas has 12 94 miles of road for every 100 square miles of territory, while the whole United States has only 6.82. Kansas has 67.27 miles of line for every 10,000 inhabitants, while the United States has only 25.76. The assessed value of these roads is $60,000,000. Operating over these roads, and doing a lucrative business are five express companies. Their business being wholly out of proportion to the tangible property they own, makes them a peculiarly difficult subject of taxation. In connection with these express and railroad transportation facilities should be mentioned the growth and prominence of the telegraph, the telephone, and the interurban electric car lines. The sleeping car and refrigerator car business may also well be mentioned as adding complexity to the income-producing property of the State.

Manufacturing is rapidly developing in Kansas and bids fair to rival the importance of agriculture, so far as the capital employed in each and the value of the product are concerned. The State ranks seventh in agriculture, but sixteenth in manufacturing: the *per capita* product of the former in 1900 was $143; of the latter, $117. The growth and present status of the manufacturing industry can be seen by a glance at the following table:

MANUFACTURING IN KANSAS.[3]

	1900	1890	1880
Number of establishments..........	7,830	4,471	2,803
Capital invested..................	$66,827,362	$43,926,002	$11,192,315
Value of product..................	$172,129,398	$110,219,805	$30,893,777
Per cent. of population wage-earners in manufacturing............	2.4 per cent	2 per cent	1.2 per cent

To show the particular lines of development followed by manufacturing in Kansas, seven selected industries are given, in the order of their importance:

1. SLAUGHTERING AND MEAT PACKING.	1900	1890
Number of establishments....................	14	18
Capital invested...........................	$16,486,177	$11,086,058

2. FLOUR AND GRIST MILLS.		
Number of establishments....................	533	348
Capital invested...........................	$8,366,966	$7,844,280

3. ZINC SMELTING AND REFINING.		
Number of establishments....................	11	4
Capital invested...........................	$5,218,529	$218,000

4. CAR SHOPS.		
Number of establishments....................	37	26
Capital invested...........................	$2,931,699	$1,683,210

5. FOUNDRY AND MACHINE SHOPS.		
Number of establishments....................	94	69
Capital invested...........................	$2,450,324	$2,624,807

6. DAIRY PRODUCTS MADE IN FACTORIES.		
Number of establishments....................	171	101
Capital invested...........................	$1,139,595	$433,792

7. SOAP AND CANDLES.		
Number of establishments....................	7	9
Capital invested...........................	$947,182	$130,379

---

[3] *Report on manufacturing.*   12 Census.

This is perhaps sufficient to indicate one line of development in the differentiation of Kansas industries. It is plainly one of increasing importance and hence due cognizance must be taken of it. Some of the industries above show a very interesting tendency towards greater concentration.

The business of mining in Kansas is a comparatively new industry, but one of no insignificant proportions. Especially is this true as regards the mining of bituminous coal. A brief record of this may be tabulated from the statistical abstracts of the United States.

COAL MINED IN KANSAS.

1880	763,597 tons	(2,240 pound-tons)
1890	2,017,788 tons	
1895	2,613,277 tons	
1900	3,989,170 tons	
1901	4,375,471 tons	
1902	4,701,844 tons	

Zinc mines yield some 100,000,000 pounds of ore annually having a value of one and one-third million dollars; and the product of lead is about 15,000,000 pounds a year, with a value of one-third of a million dollars. Other industries of importance in this class are salt and oil. These are all to be reckoned with in any rational system of taxation which aims to deal fairly with different classes of property.

To complete this representation of the more prominent features of the taxable field of the State, mention must be made of a few forms of personal property. These do not constitute a separate category, strictly speaking, but do not happen to be included in any of the foregoing enumerations. Reference is had to the various forms of intangible personalty, such as mortgages, notes, stocks, bonds, etc., which common observation teaches are becoming every year more important elements of individual property. They constitute a factor in the taxable capacity of the State, and hence will be treated in their proper place. This discussion has not followed the simple division into real and personal property because as a classification it is outgrown and unsatisfactory, and entirely inadequate to present needs.

Having taken this preliminary survey of the field, we are now ready to enter upon the financial history of Kansas.

CHAPTER II

TERRITORIAL FINANCES—1854–1861

The seven years of Kansas' territorial life were a period of storm and stress. It is not necessary at this point to recount the fierce and bloody free-state struggle which culminated in the admission of the State into the Union free from the incubus of slavery. Territorial finances very naturally shared the vicissitudes and uncertainties of the political contest.

The "Organic Act" of Congress in 1854, more generally known as the Kansas–Nebraska bill, provided a territorial government of the usual form for Kansas. Congress, realizing the privations of frontier life, adopted the policy of paying from the national treasury the initial territorial and legislative expenses, the policy of erecting public buildings, appropriating lands for schools and colleges, and of permitting the emigrant to settle upon the public lands free from taxation until a full title should be acquired. The Organic Act empowered the president of the United States to appoint all the officers of the executive and judicial departments of the Territory, and provided for a popular election, at the call of the governor, of the legislative branch, that is, the Council and House of Representatives. The only specific provision concerning finance in the Act was that no tax should be imposed upon the property of the United States, nor should the lands or other property of non-residents be taxed higher than the property of residents. Beyond this, the inhabitants were free to regulate their financial affairs as they saw fit. To equip and start the new government on its way, the president named the necessary appointees, and Congress, in 1855, made an appropriation of $64,700. Of this sum, $25,000 was to be used for public buildings; the balance covered the salaries of the executive and judicial officers, contingent expenses, and the expenses of a legislative assembly, census, election of a delegate to the federal House of Representatives, and a territorial library.[1]

Kansas, already at this early period, represented two distinct parties—the Pro-slavery and the Free-state. The first election accordingly, called by Governor A. H. Reeder, a man of anti-slavery principles, precipitated a conflict which was destined to cost dearly in both property and human life before it merged into the great national struggle of the Civil war. This first election was carried by voters from Missouri, and the so-called Bogus Legislature came into power, enjoying the favor and sanction of the federal administration.[2] They moved the seat of government from Pawnee, near the center of the Territory, to Shawnee Mission, a point near the Missouri line, a spot more convenient to the homes of the legislators. This was done in defiance of the governor who had, in accordance with law, chosen the temporary seat of government. This move, the legislators claimed, was forced upon them, for the reason that at Pawnee there was no place of accommodation, and members had to camp out, sleep in their wagons or tents, and cook their own provisions.[3] At Shawnee Mission a house was rented and an appropriation made therefor from the contingent fund. An elaborate code of laws, based on the Missouri statutes, was enacted. The objects of taxation, the chapter on revenue declared, should be the support of the government of the Territory, the payment of the public debt, and the advancement of the public welfare.[4] No further refinements or distinctions were thought necessary. Taxes were to be levied on land and improvements, leaseholds, slaves, and all personalty, including money and credits. And, to put the stamp of their generous spirit on the laws, the legislators provided for the exemption from taxation of the "property of all widows and minors who are not worth more than $1,000." As a secondary tax, but what afterwards proved to be

---

[1] Library, $5,000; census, $2,000; election of delegate, $700; legislative assembly, $20,000; salaries of governor. three judges, and secretary, $10,500; contingent expenses, $1,500; capitol, $25,000.
[2] *Report of the Special Committee on the troubles in Kansas,* No. 200. H. R., 34 Cong., 1 Sess. 1856.
[3] *Statutes of Ter. of Kansas.* 1 Sess. Legislative Assembly, 1855, p. vi ff.
[4] *Statutes of 1855,* ch. 137.

the chief source of revenue, there was levied an easily collectible poll tax on men from 21 to 55 years old. This tax varied from 50 cents to $1, as the need required. Provision was also made for a duty on the proceeds of auction sales, for a license on auctioneers, and for licenses on peddlers of all kinds, book-peddlers alone excepted. These were but minor sources of revenue, however, to the territorial treasury. A fee system was inaugurated, applying to offices where the time and amount of services were uncertain,[5] such as the district attorney, county commissioners, judge of probate court, clerk of supreme court, clerk of district court, sheriff, coroner, constable, justice of the peace, notary public, and recorder.

A crude form of self-assessment was also provided, whereby the county assessor, chosen yearly by the county tribunal, was to designate a certain point in each township where the people were to come in and hand to him written lists of all their property. It is almost superfluous to add that this impotent system soon fell into disuse.

There was also an interesting section of this revenue law pertaining to the taxation of corporations, typical of all subsequent legislation on this subject by reason of its lumping all corporations together in an undifferentiated mass. The section in question provides for tapping the corporations at the source, rather than the distributed shares of stock. ''Persons owning shares of stock,'' says this law, ''in banks and other incorporated companies, taxable by law, are not required to deliver to the assessor a list thereof, but the president or other chief officer of such corporation shall deliver to the assessor a list of all shares of stock held therein, and the names of the persons who hold the same. The tax assessed on shares of stock embraced in such list shall be paid by the corporators respectively.''

The sheriff was the collector of revenues for a few years, and then this duty was assigned to the county treasurer. The rate of local taxation was limited to twice the territorial rate on the same subject, and this was meant, of course, to curtail local activities. The fines and penalties in each county were to be applied to the support of the common schools.

---

[5] *Statutes of 1855*, ch. 119.

This is, in brief, the crude revenue system which the Bogus Legislature attempted to superimpose upon the young territory. But with a population of only 8,601 souls in the Territory, it is evident that no system could have succeeded in raising much revenue. Each succeeding territorial legislature modified the revenue laws in many particulars and added entirely new sections. Soon territorial and county boards of equalization appear. Exemption was made to apply to $200 worth of personalty, and to all the property of "persons infirm, old, poor, etc., unable to contribute;" and then a little later only to the property of widows to the amount of $500. Just debts were to be subtracted from personal property. The matter of exemptions, it is worthy of note, formed one of the most perplexing things for adjustment, not only at this time, but later. The question of the redemption of land sold for taxes was also a much mooted point. This was finally left by the territorial law givers to a three-year limit, with interest at the rate of 25 per cent. on all back taxes paid and other costs incurred by the tax-title purchaser. Other minor points in the revenue laws were changed from year to year, for this process of tampering with the tax laws, once begun, was never discontinued.

The workings of these revenue laws may well claim our attention at this point. As far as these earliest laws are concerned, it is to be remembered that the members of the Bogus Legislature overreached themselves in the matter of their law-making, especially on the delicate subject of slavery. The law on this subject, in 1855, is certainly a most conspicuous record of human greed, malevolence and tyranny. It provided that any person advising insurrection among the negroes or assisting in the circulation of any paper for the purpose of exciting revolt on the part of slaves or free negroes should be punished with death, and that any person maintaining it was wrong to hold slaves in this territory should be imprisoned at least two years, and that any person conscientiously opposed to holding slaves should not sit as juror in a trial for the violation of any of the provisions of this act.[6]

A legislature capable of passing such a law as this was *not*

---

[6] *Statutes of Kansas*, 1855, ch. 151.

capable of compelling respect and obedience to this or any other of its acts in Kansas Territory, peopled as it then was, with northern men principally. So its revenue laws were inoperative and ineffectual. so far as free-state men were concerned.

Opposition soon became open and organized. For instance, we read in a contemporary newspaper of Lawrence. Kansas, an account of a public meeting held for the purpose of consulting over the assessment and payment of taxes said to be levied upon them by the Bogus Legislature.[7] Among other things, it was unanimously resolved, "that we recommend to our oppressors that if they are out of money and must have a little to replenish their stock of—whiskey, that they levy their Tax upon their constituents of Missouri, and let honest men support a government of their own choice.

"On motion Resolved. that the papers of Lawrence be requested to publish the proceedings of this meeting."

Thus we see the spirit and temper of the people, when it came to a question of lending financial support to the alien legislature. But fortunately this body continued in power but two years.

Territorial auditors very naturally complained that counties were slow in responding to the officials of the Territory. The only source of revenue, to speak of, was the poll tax. In the years 1856. 1857, and 1858 delinquent taxes swelled to $27,298. The legislature of 1858, succeeding the Bogus Legislature, fixing the rate of the territorial tax, provided that no part of the new tax should be appropriated towards paying the old debts of the Territory. The auditor recommended the collection of the old taxes, however, that they might be applied on new debts. When the 1860 legislature convened in January of that year, only 11 out of 30 counties had reported their 1859 assessment, hence the auditor was unable to report the taxable property of the Territory to the legislature. He says, after speaking of this fact: "Neither can I report to you anything like a correct estimate of the probable expenses of the territorial government for the ensuing year, as you are well aware this will much de-

---

[7] *Herald of Freedom*, June 20, 1857.

pend upon your legislation, and therefore cannot be foreseen or estimated by the auditor.''[8]

The free-state men never paid a cent of the tax levied by the Bogus Legislature.[9] It remained charged against the respective counties, constantly accumulating by interest, until 1867, when the State Legislature canceled it. The counties were very slow about paying their regularly levied taxes, and used the expedient of returning a delinquent list from year to year with their territorial taxes, thus throwing their deficits onto the territorial treasury.

We see from the foregoing that the sources of territorial revenue were extremely precarious. The operations of the territorial government, however, were merely of a temporary and tentative character, otherwise they would have been seriously crippled. Constitution making was the chief activity and admission into the Union was the one goal. The question of permanent improvements was postponed till after the acquisition of statehood. Even the $25,000 appropriated by Congress for the erection of a capitol was squandered, leaving nothing to show for it but a stone foundation in the little country village of Lecompton.

An examination of the territorial budget shows that the four chief objects of expenditure in the order of their importance were: (1) Investigation of election frauds; (2) Holding constitutional conventions; (3) Territorial roads; (4) Legislative expenses. Revenue was far too small to meet the warrants drawn on the treasury. By the auditor's reports, we see the situation was as follows:

YEAR	REVENUE	WARRANTS
1855		$398 00
1856	$1,811 88	3,170 60
1857	3,383 09	13,287 55
1858	681 12	4,502 93
1859	25,544 06	62,409 26
1860	3,197 53	41,234 14
1861		10,467 88
	$34,617 68	$135,470 16

[8] *Council Journal, K. T.,* 1860, p. 14.
[9] Holloway, *Hist. of Kansas,* p. 437.

These warrants were all issued under "acts making appropriations," and hence have nothing to do with the "claims" which constituted an enormous debt in themselves, as explained below. The floating debt created by these warrants proved very harassing to the Territory. An unsuccessful attempt was made to unload it on Congress, but Congress at this time had more serious matters on hand. After a few years' delay the State government accepted it and issued bonds enough to fund it.

The matter of the claims alluded to above forms an interesting chapter in the Territory's history. They were the natural heritage of the border troubles, now so familiar to every student of those stirring times. In the early years of the Territory a great many claims were presented to the legislature for indemnity for moneys spent in maintaining the laws of the Territory, suppressing rebellion, furnishing military supplies, and for loss of property by depredations.[10] Provision was made for fully and correctly ascertaining these losses. So complete was the investigation, and so fully did it reveal the fearful character of the troubles endured by the settlers during two of their stormiest years, that the whole mass of testimony was published by order of Congress, making two large volumes, of 892 pages each.

The territorial statute of 1859, covering these claims was ambiguous, implying that they were to be paid by Congress, but stating that the auditor was to issue his warrant on the treasurer for each claim allowed by the Claims Commission.[11] The auditor accordingly drew warrants for $380,774.13. The treasurer issued territorial bonds on the face of these warrants to the amount of $95,700, the law limiting the funded debt to $100,000. The last territorial legislature took up the matter, and enthusiastically voted to repudiate the whole debt, both warrants and bonds. And almost in the next breath, both Houses, in a concurrent resolution, voted to memorialize Congress for a grant on these same claims, either of 500,000 acres of land, or $500,000 in money. To settle the fate of these claims, so far as their payment by Kansas was concerned, the incoming State legislature promptly made their repudition definite and abso-

10 House Journal, K. T., 1861, p. 273-312.
11 House Journal, K. T., 1861, p. 316-347, 482. Council Journal, p. 304.

Iute.[12] Congress ignored the subject entirely, and so the holders of the claims were doomed to complete disappointment.

The history of the four constitutions before the people of the Territory is worthy of note, constituting as they did the one great issue of territorial politics. Their history may be summarized as follows:

(1) The Topeka Constitution, adopted December 15, 1855, by the inhabitants of the Territory. The pro-slavery men did not vote, and Congress rejected this constitution.

(2) Lecompton Constitution, rejected (second time) January 4, 1858, on a full vote.

(3) The Leavenworth Constitution died before the legislature, 1858.

(4) Wyandotte Constitution, adopted July 29, 1859, and accepted by Congress. Kansas admitted to the Union under this constitution, January 29, 1861.

The State paid the heavy expenses connected with the conventions framing the unsuccessful Lecompton and Leavenworth constitutions, and the successful Wyandotte constitution, but the Topeka convention was looked upon as an extra-legal affair. Its story is a very brief one. The Bogus Legislature had been ignored by the free-state men, who determined to forestall further usurpations by adopting a constitution and securing its acceptance by Congress. Accordingly a delegate convention was held at Topeka in the latter part of 1855, in which an executive committee was appointed with certain powers of a provisional government, looking forward to the formation of a State constitution and government. According to the report of the investigating committee chosen later on, this executive committee conducted its business in a prudent, judicious, economical, and masterly manner.[13] With that miscalculating optimism which marked so much of the subsequent political career of their successors, these men issued scrip to meet their expenses. They received it themselves as pay for their services, as did likewise the members of the Topeka Constitutional Convention which met soon afterwards. The people also received the scrip at its full

[12] *Laws of Kansas*, 1861, ch. 5.
[13] Prouty, *Topeka Constitutional Scrip*. Pamphlet, Topeka, 1887.

valuation. Thousands of dollars of it were cashed at par by friends of Kansas—the East. The Topeka constitution was adopted by a large majority of the popular vote, but the pro-slavery element took no part in the election. The free-state men thought their cause was won. A governor and legislature were soon chosen, and three short sessions of the legislature held under the Topeka constitution. But federal troops dispersed the assembly, the governor was arrested on a charge of treason, and Congress, after long deliberation, rejected this constitution. And thus this honest effort at "squatter sovereignty" was ef-fectually stifled. Some $25,000 in scrip had been issued by the Executive Committee and the Topeka government together, and an act thoughtfully passed providing that the State should redeem this scrip. But statehood failed to come just when ex-pected. The holders of the scrip waited until admission as a State, and long years afterwards, for some action to be taken in the matter, resting satisfied as to the justice of their claims. An unsuccessful effort was made in 1883 to secure redemption by the State, and again four years later, but with no better results. Holders of the scrip had become too few and feeble. In the early days of statehood, the State had been too poor to pay these claims; when it became rich enough, it had no desire to pay them.

Railroads.—The railroads of Kansas have played too import-ant a rôle in her development and financial history to be neg-lected in a discussion of this kind. For the question of grant-ing subsidies to these roads has continued a live issue up to the present time.

At the very first session of the territorial legislature, in 1855, there were incorporated five railroad companies, a large number certainly for 8,000 people. The zeal of the incorporators, how-ever, was not so much for constructing roads as for securing valuable territorial franchises, as was evidenced by their subse-quent conduct. In the cases of some of these roads, the Leaven-worth, Pawnee and Western, for example, county courts were authorized to subscribe for stock and issue county bonds in pay-ment thereof.[14] The sentiment of the people was voiced by the

---

[14] *Statutes of K. T. 1855*, ch. 86, sec. 15.

Leavenworth Journal of this time, speaking of a prospective road. "If the road is to be built at all," says the *Journal*, "the brunt must be borne by Leavenworth. Unless our reported wealth is fictitious there can be no doubt as to our ability to do all that will be required of us to secure this road."[15]

But no railroad was built till after the territorial period. All grants of franchises, etc., of course, held over under the State laws.

Banking.—Territorial banking remained also undeveloped, although the legislature of 1857 incorporated a giant bank with an authorized capital of $800,000, subscriptions to be paid in gold and silver. Authority was also granted to establish five branch banks, each with a capital of $300,000, and with the same powers as the main bank. Each was to issue paper to the limit of $3 in paper for every $1 of specie on hand. This system of course was far in excess of the actual need of the territory, and was never carried out as planned.[16]

---

[15] *Leavenworth Journal*, Aug. 26, 1858.
[16] *Laws of Kans. Terr. 1857*, Second Session, p. 103.

CHAPTER III

CONSTITUTIONAL PROVISIONS

Kansas was admitted into the Union January 29, 1861, under the so-called Wyandotte constitution. A study of the genesis of this constitution shows that its framers based the financial provisions in it on the Ohio constitution of 1851, and to a less extent, on the Wisconsin constitution of 1848. The section concerning lotteries in the Ohio constitution is borrowed in the Kansas document.

To this constitution, as it went before Congress, was prefixed an "Ordinance" and subjoined a set of "Resolutions." The constitution was sandwiched between these two statements for forcing them, apparently, on the attention of Congress, and giving them more weight before that body. In the Ordinance, which is an interesting set of statements, Kansas promised forever to forego the right to tax the government lands in the state if the Government would, in turn, meet the following modest conditions:

(1) Grant to the State for her common schools, (a) sections 16 and 36 in each township (of 36 sections); (b) 500,000 acres of land as per act of Congress September 4, 1841; (c) and 5 per cent. of the proceeds of public lands of the State.

(2) Grant to the State, as University lands, 72 sections.

(3) Grant to the State for public buildings, 36 sections.

(4) Grant to the State for benevolent institutions, 72 sections.

(5) Grant to the State for works of public improvement 12 salt springs with 72 sections of land.

These propositions were laid down as conditions for the general government to accept, although it certainly did not fall within the province of the young candidate for statehood to impose any conditions whatever upon Congress.

After the concluding section of the constitution some more wants were made known, but not in the lofty tone of conditions as stated in the Ordinance preceding. This time they were humbly stated as requests under the caption of "Resolutions." Under these Resolutions Congress was *requested:*

(1) To grant to the State 4,500,000 acres of land to aid in the construction of railroads and other internal improvements.

(2) To appropriate 50,000 acres of land for the improvement of the Kansas river from its mouth to Fort Riley. (This is an interesting request. seeing that Fort Riley is 140 miles from the mouth of the river, and for years there has been a dam across this stream at Lawrence, 40 miles from its mouth.)

(3) To grant all swamp lands to the State for the benefit of the common schools.

(4) To appropriate $500,000, or in lieu thereof, 500,000 acres of land, for the payment of territorial claims (Acts of 1859).

(5) To assume the territorial debt.

As was to be expected, Congress coolly ignored both the Ordinance and Resolutions, and in turn. offered certain propositions to the people of Kansas.[1] These propositions, however, covered in part the points adduced in the Ordinance, and were all accepted by the Kansas legislature.[2] These grants, while not so munificent as those received by some neighboring States, were of considerable importance to the welfare of Kansas. They were:

(1) For common schools, sections 16 and 36 in each township.

(2) For a State University, 72 sections.

(3) For public buildings. 10 sections.

(4) Twelve Salt Springs, for use as the Legislature might see fit.

(5) Five per cent. of the sales of public lands, for making

---

[1] Congress, Act of Admission. See *Genl. Stat. Kans. 1901.* p. 1, ff., for Organic Act, Kansas Constitution, Ordinance, Resolutions, etc., etc.

[2] Joint Resolution. *Laws of Kans. 1862.* Jan. 20.

public roads and internal improvements, or for other purposes, as the Legislature might direct.

These gifts were all applied as foundations for the educational work of the State, except the small grant for public buildings, which was used to aid in the erection of the capitol. And, it should be added, the 500,000 acres, under the Congressional grant of 1841, was also placed—for a while—to the credit of the schools.

The foregoing provisions of Congress were merely incidental to the State constitution. To the constitution itself we must look for all those definite, rigid provisions which govern subsequent legislation on financial subjects. These provisions stand as an almost impassable barrier today in the way of any change, whether good or bad. The financial sections of the constitution may be classified under these headings: (1) revenue; (2) debt; (3) treasury; (4) school funds; (5) internal improvement; (6) lottery; (7) banking; and (8) miscellany.

(1) *Revenue.*—Bills for raising revenue may originate in either house, but may be amended or rejected by the other.[3] "Finance and Taxation" are treated together as one subject, for the State income contemplated by the constitution is primarily a direct, general property tax. Uniformity is the key note in the rule of taxation and exemption which states, "The legislature shall provide for a uniform and equal rate of assessment and taxation; but all property used exclusively for State, county, municipal, literary, educational, scientific, religious, benevolent and charitable purposes, and personal property to the amount of at least $200 for each family, shall be exempted from taxation."[4] A *uniform* and an *equal* rate of assessment meant one and the same thing when this provision was inserted in the constitution, but subsequent changes in the character of taxable property made a *uniform* assessment an *unequal* one, as will be shown in a later chapter. It proved a case of equal treatment of unequals. Banks were the only corporations thought worthy of especial mention under the tax provisions of the constitution. These were treated as follows.[5] "The legis-

---

[3] *Constitution of Kansas.* Art. 2, Sec. 12.
[4] Art. 11, Sec. 1.
[5] Art. 11, Sec. 2.

lature shall provide for taxing the notes and bills discounted or purchased, moneys loaned, and other property, effects or dues of every description (without deduction) of all banks now existing, or hereafter to be created, and of all bankers; so that all property employed in banking shall always bear a burden of taxation equal to that imposed upon the property of individuals.'' We see in this provision some lingering apprehensions of unknown dangers of a great moneyed monopoly dating back to those historical experiences of our own and other countries with money-issuing institutions.

The rule governing the time for which appropriations shall be made is similar to that in the Federal constitution. "The legislature shall provide at each regular session, for raising revenue sufficient to defray the current expenses of the State for two years. No tax shall be levied except in pursuance of a law, which shall distinctly state the object of the same, to which object only such tax shall be applied. * * * No appropriation shall be for a longer term than two years.''[5]

(2) *Debt.*—Bankruptcy and debt repudiation in the eastern States had given sufficient warning to the framers of the Kansas constitution. Accordingly we find certain limits laid down for the State debt. For the purpose of defraying extraordinary expenses and making public improvements, the State may contract a debt of $1,000,000. Adequate provision must be made at the time the debt is contracted for the payment of interest and principal when due. No debt of over $1,000,000 may be contracted without first submitting the question to a popular vote at a general election and securing a majority in its favor.

It is further provided in another section,[6] that the State may borrow money to repel invasion, suppress insurrection, or defend the State in time of war, but the money thus raised shall be applied exclusively to the object for which the loan was authorized, or to the repayment of the debt thereby created. So, as a matter of fact, the State may in time of war contract a debt beyond the million-dollar limit without submitting it to a popular vote.

---

[5] Art. 11, Sec. 3, 4; Art. 2, Sec. 24.
[6] Art. 11, Sec. 5, 6, 7.

(3) *Treasury.*—Only two provisions pertain to the treasury administration. No money shall be drawn from the treasury except in pursuance of a specific appropriation, and an accurate, detailed statement of all receipts and expenditures of the public moneys shall be published as prescribed by law.[7]

(4) *School Funds.*—Considerable attention is paid in the constitution to these funds, provisions being made both for funds of the University and of the common schools. Their sources as well as their management are covered by general regulations. Regarding the sources, the constitution says, "the proceeds of all lands that have been, or may be granted by the United States to the State, for the support of schools, and the 500,000 acres of land granted to the new States, under an act of Congress distributing the proceeds of public lands among the several States of the union, approved September 4, 1841, and all estates of persons dying without heir or will, and such per cent. as may be granted by Congress of the sale of lands in the State, shall be the common property of the State, and shall be a perpetual school fund, which shall not be diminished, but the interest of which, together with all rents of the lands, and such other means as the legislature may provide by tax or otherwise, shall be inviolably appropriated to the support of common schools."[8] Provision is also made for augmenting the annual common school funds of the municipalities by this inclusive section:[9] "All money which shall be paid by persons as an equivalent for exemption from military duty, the clear proceeds of estrays, ownership of which shall vest in the taker-up; and the proceeds of fines for any breach of the penal law, shall be exclusively applied, in the several counties in which the money is paid or fines collected, to the support of the common schools."

All funds arising from the sale of university lands, and all other grants or bequests, either by the State or by individuals, for the university, shall remain a perpetual fund, to be called the university fund, and the interest of which shall be appropriated to the support of the State University.[10]

---

[7] Art. 2, Sec. 24 ; Art. 13, Sec. 5.
[8] Art. 6, Sec. 3.
[9] Art. 6. Sec. 6.
[10] Art. 6, Sec. 7.

For the management and investment of the school funds of the State, a board of commissioners is created, consisting of the state superintendent of public instruction, the secretary of state, and the attorney general.[11] The income of these funds is to be disbursed annually to the several school districts according to the number of children of school age (5 to 21 years), and where school is held at least three months in the year.[12]

The framers of the constitution weighed the proposition of making the school lands a part of the permanent patrimony of the State. The following flexible proposition was, however, adopted: ''The school lands shall not be sold unless such sale shall be authorized by a vote of the people at a general election; but, subject to a revaluation every five years, they may be leased for any number of years, not exceeding 25, at a rate established by law.''[13]

Concerning ecclesiastical management of public school moneys, it is provided that ''no religious sect or sects shall ever control any part of the common school or university funds of the State.''[14]

(5) *Internal Improvement.*—The statement on this subject is brief and concise.[15] The ''State shall never be a party in carrying on any works of internal improvement.''

(6) *Lotteries.*—''Lotteries and the sale of lottery tickets are forever prohibited.''[16] Thus this revenue scheme was peremptorily thrust aside. the social considerations involved being held paramount to its possible fiscal advantages.

(7) *Banking.*—Many constitutional provisions on the subject of banking clearly pertain only to banks of issue, and hence were rendered obsolete by the United States National Bank acts of 1863 and 1864. These are therefore omitted here. Other sections are not so clear, as, for instance, the following:[17] ''No bank shall be established otherwise than under a general banking law. The State shall not be a stockholder in any banking institution. No banking law shall be in force until the same shall have been submitted to a vote of the electors of the State at some

---

[11] Art. 6, Sec. 9.
[12] Art. 6, Sec. 4.
[13] Art. 6, Sec. 5.
[14] Art. 6, Sec. 8.

[15] Art. 11, Sec. 8.
[16] Art. 15, Sec. 3.
[17] Art. 13, Sec. 1, 5, 8.

general election, and approved by a majority of all the votes cast.''

The courts settled the question of the interpretation of these sections a few years after the adoption of the constitution. It was held that this entire article on banking applied only to banks of issues, and did not prohibit the legislature from creating banks of deposit and discount.[18]

(8) *Miscellany.*—The only limitations concerning municipal taxation are found in this elastic section: ''Provision shall be made by general law for the organization of cities, towns, and villages; and their powers of taxation, assessment, borrowing money, contracting debts, and loaning their credit, shall be so restricted as to prevent the abuse of such power.''[19] Thus we see the municipalities have no specific constitutional limits set to their indebtedness, whereas the State is limited to $1,000,000, practically.

Public printing, one of the most important items in the State budget, is regulated by a clause in the constitution, declaring it shall be done at the capital by a State printer elected by the legislature in joint session.[20] This remains, therefore, one of the choicest bits of patronage at the disposal of the State legislature.

Under the miscellaneous provisions of the constitution, we find one section vesting the legislature with anomalous judicial and administrative powers over the salaries of certain officers. ''The legislature,'' says this section, ''may reduce the salaries of officers who shall neglect the performance of any legal duty.''[21]

The foregoing are all of the provisions of the constitution pertaining specifically or generally to financial matters. Legislation has for the most part conformed to these regulations, but not always. The most violent departures have come before the courts for correction, but many minor irregularities have never been subjected to judicial scrutiny.

It now remains to trace the development of Kansas finances under this constitution, and this will be done in the following pages.

---

[18] 20 *Kans.*, 440.
[19] Art. 12, Sec. 5.

[20] Art. 15, Sec. 4.
[21] Art. 15, Sec. 7.

CHAPTER IV

NINE YEARS OF CREDIT FINANCIERING, 1861–1869

While Secretary Chase was grappling with the problems of federal finances just before the impending crisis of the great Civil War, the young commonwealth of Kansas was beginning to face serious financial questions of her own. Hardships were doubly great, because it was a period of beginnings as well as a period of war. The late territory had bequeathed nothing to the young State, except a heritage of debt. There was no building for the State legislature to meet in; no charitable institutions for defective and dependent; no penitentiary for the violators of the law. All these were to be provided at once. Aid was pressingly needed by the general government in raising troops and making other military preparations, and in this extremity a direct tax of over $70,000 had been imposed upon the State. And, to make matters worse, the outgoing territorial government had "signalized its dissolution by stamping upon its credit the ineffaceable stigma of repudiation, thus leaving the new State without funds for the payment of current expenses, and also excluded from those money markets which are the ordinary resources [sic] of needy governments."[1]

Tax Laws.—The tax laws of this period continued that process of alteration and mending which was begun early in territorial days. Change followed change too rapidly for any measure to be thoroughly tested, or for officers to adapt themselves to the new conditions. The second governor claimed that on the subject of taxation he had neither statistics nor facts.[2]

---

[1] First *Auditor's Report.* 1861. *Kans. Doc.,* 1861.
[2] *Inaugural Message of Gov. Carney,* 1863.

We will examine briefly the nature of the tax laws of this period before proceeding with the discussion of the State income.

The subject of exemptions was one that underwent the fewest changes at this time. Legislators were satisfied to leave the amount exempt from taxation at $200 of personalty for each family and those other classes of property of a public nature specifically mentioned in the constitution. The true value in money was designated as the legal rule for valuing all property. Merchants and manufacturers were to be taxed on the average value of their stock on hand during the preceding year. Banks and bankers were to be taxed once at the bank for all the stock of the bank. "Railways and other corporations" formed an independent category of property and were to make sworn returns of tangible property to the various county clerks, and on this self-assessment were to be taxed. Real estate according to the 1863 law, was to be assessed every three years. This was changed three years later to a yearly assessment. County and state boards of equalization were made a part of the system. Attempt was made to reach all personal property by having returns made as stated by the owner, supplemented with a double oath—that of the owner and that of the assessor. This, it was hoped, would prevent all forms of lying and collusion. A satisfactory rule for the levy of taxes was adopted which provided that the levy should be made by a board of county commissioners for the county, by the mayor and council for cities, and by a school board for school districts. Both land and personal property were to be sold for unpaid taxes, under certain conditions. The provisions for redemption of lands thus sold were subjects of much controversy. The time limit for redemption was left at three years, but the per cent. to be added to the sale-price, taxes, and other expenses was hard to settle satisfactorily. Too large a per cent. bore heavily on the debtor whose lands had been sold by the sheriff at a tax sale. And too low a per cent. caused carelessness and negligence on the delinquent's part, a very disastrous thing to the local revenues. Twenty-five per cent. was thought a proper penalty for several years, but results were disappointing.

Plenty of cheap land favored mobility of farmers. In 1869˙ this penalty was raised to 50 per cent.[3]

The amount of tinkering with the tax laws shows they were a misfit in many ways. The situation was well summed up by Governor Carney in his message of 1864, when he wrote, "I declare the simple truth when I say that the first tax system adopted by each western State, and by the cities in each western state, was bad—so bad that its very abuses compelled an entire reform. * * * Now, if we were to act in our representative capacity as individuals do who adapt themselves practically to new circumstances, we would, instead of remembering the ways and customs of our old homes, thrown by as cast-off clothes, examine the best ways of taxation, and adopt one equal to the best. This is the course I recommend to you as being alike practical and wise. Let all protected by the State share equally its burdens in proportion to their property."

Income.—Having taken this brief survey of the tax laws of this period, we are now in a position to consider the State income, depending as it did on the successful working of these laws. The needs of the State, however, being unusually great, and the tax system being rather a tentative scheme than a successful system, it follows necessarily that the bulk of state revenues had to come from other sources than taxation, *i. e.*, loans.

The State tax levy during this period was higher than was ever reached afterwards. But collections were slow. The legislature frequently extended the time one year for a county to collect its taxes. This was done in 1861 in the case of Leavenworth, Breckenridge, Lykins and other counties. Whenever counties made a mistake and returned erroneous or double-assessments, this was subtracted from their apportionment, or else charged against the State as a debt to the counties. This threw the loss on the State and off the county where it belonged. The amount of these taxes which the State was thus called on to refund to the counties was an important item and contributed not a little towards deranging the State's finances.

---

[3] See *Session Laws,* 1869; also *Genl. Statutes,* 1868, ch. 107; *Session Laws,* 1866, ch. 118; 1863, ch. 60.

The treasurers' reports of this period exhibit the amount and high rates of the State levy, as is shown in the table below:

TOTAL ASSESSED VALUATION, LEVY, AND RATE OF STATE TAXES.

Year.	Valuation.	Levy.	Rate in mills.
1861	$24,737.563	$14,234	4
1862	19,285,749	115,737	8
1863	25,460,499	152,763	7
1864	30,502,791	182,585	7
1865	36,120,945	216,757	7
1866	50,439,645	252,201	6
1867	56,276,360	281,382	6
1868	66,949,950	435,408	6½
1869	76,333,697	763,837	10

In addition to the first year's levy of four mills, a poll tax of fifty cents was levied upon every white male between the ages of 21 and 50 years.

This income from taxation was inadequate to meet current expenses, not to speak of the extraordinary expenses of public buildings, and the military expenses in connection with the war. Hence recourse had to be had to the sale of bonds, and on such terms as the State's credit could command. Since part of these bonds were for military purposes—"to repel invasion, suppress insurrection and defend the State" in the language of the Act, the million-dollar limit was not observed. Several different bond issues were made, for the various purposes before mentioned, aggregating $1,373,275, and bearing interest at rates from 6 to 10 per cent. A few were sold in the local home market in small blocks at par, but far the greater portion were disposed of in New York in large amounts and at heavy discounts.

Later bond issues sink into insignificance when compared with this period of nine years. During the next thirty years, the entire amount of bonds issued on new debts was almost exactly one twenty-eighth of the issue of these nine years. For, up to the year 1900, omitting the refunding of these early bonds, only $49,000 of bonds were issued. Hence it is that this period stands out so strikingly as one of credit financiering.

The particulars of sale, rates of interest, etc., of these bonds will be readily seen by a glance at the following table:

BOND STATEMENT, 1861-1869.

Issued under act of	Date of issue.	For what.	Int. Rate per cent.	When payable.	Where.	Face of bonds.	Amount sold for.	Rate sold for.
1861	July 1. 1861	Current expenses	7	1876	N. Y.	$150,000	} $173,150 00	84.9
1863	Mch. 20,1863	Current expenses	7	1878	N. Y.	54,000		
1863	July 1, 1863	Fund Ter. Debt.	6	1883	Topeka	61,600	61,600 00	100.
1864	July 1, 1864	Refund Taxes ...	6	1884	Topeka	39,675	39,675 00	100.
1864	July 1, 1864	Military.	7	1884	N. Y.	100,000	87,586 00	87.6
1864	July 1, 1864	Penitentiary.....	7	1884	N. Y.	50,000	45,000 00	90.0
1866	July 1, 1866	Penitentiary.....	7	1886	N. Y.	60,000	54,600 00	91.0
1866	July 1, 1866	Pub.improvem'ts	7	1896	N. Y.	70,000	63,310 00	90.4
1866	July 1, 1866	Military...... ...	7	1886	Topeka	40,000	38,220 00	95.5
1867	July 1, 1867	Penitentiary....	7	1897	N. Y.	100,000	89,329 16	89.3
1867	July 1, 1867	Capitol.	7	1897	N. Y.	100,000	89,513 00	89.5
1867	July 1, 1867	Deaf & D. Asyl..	7	1887	Topeka	15,500	15,500 00	100.
1868	July 1, 1868	Capitol.........	7	1898	N. Y.	150,000	137,180 00	91.4
1868	July 1, 1868	Penitentiary.....	7	1898	N. Y.	50,000	45,588 35	91.1
1868	July 1, 1868	Military	7	1888	N. Y.	30,000	27,353 00	91.1
1868	July 1. 1868	Insane Asyl......	7	1898	N. Y.	20,000	18,352 33	91.7
1869	Jan. 1, 1869	Military.........	7	1889	N. Y.	75,000	69.000 00	92.0
1869	Jan. 1, 1869	Military.........	7	1899	N. Y.	89,000	83,200 00	93.5
1869	Jan. 1, 1869	Military.........	7	1889	N. Y.	12,000	11,380 00	94.8
1869	Jan. 1, 1869	Capitol..........	7	1889	N. Y.	70,000	66,442 57	94.9
1861	July 1, 1862	Military..........	10	1863	....	31,000	12,400 00	40.
1866	April 1, 1866	Ag. College.	10	1871	....	5,500	5,500 00	100.
		Totals........			....	$1,373,275	$1,233,679 41	89.

Average amount sold for, 89 per cent.

The first bond issue, that of $150,000, was an unfortunate one in many respects. It was for current expenses which should have been met by taxation. The negotiation of these bonds involved some irregularities which led to the impeachment of the governor, auditor and secretary of state. The law contemplated the sale of these bonds at 70 cents on the dollar and authorized the three men named above to carry out the details of the sale. An agent was employed under contract to sell the bonds and return to the State 60 per cent. of their face value, any surplus thereover to go to the agent as a commission. This was thought a fair price by many, while others considered 50 per cent. a good price for Kansas bonds.[4] The bond agent, however, found a good market in New York and sold a large part of the bonds at 85 per cent., but only 60 per cent. was turned into the State treasury. The cry of fraud was raised. An impeachment of the governor, auditor and secretary of the

[4] The minority report of the House Investigating Committee, 1862, thought 50 per cent. more than the market value of Kansas bonds. *House Journal*, 1862, p. 333.

state followed, in which the auditor and secretary were convicted and removed from office, but the governor, Charles Robinson, was enthusiastically acquitted.

The territorial debt was funded by issuing bonds of $100 each, putting a few on the market each year as territorial warrants came in.

Errors on the part of counties remitting their share of State taxes were successfully shifted to the public treasury, and this increased the bonded debt by about $40,000, when it came to refunding these taxes.

Of the bonds issued in 1867, the penitentiary and the capitol bonds were the principal ones, being 30-year, 7 per cent. bonds, with a total face value of $200,000. The State realized $178,842 in cash from their sale. That is, the loss in discount to the State was $21,158. The interest paid on these was, in all, $420,000, or over twice their face value. Adding this to the discount, we have the State, for the immediate use of $200,000, paying in the end, $441,158.

But a heavier burden was thrown on the State in her short-term loans. For instance, $31,000 of military bonds were negotiated and sold at 40 per cent., the bonds bearing 10 per cent. interest and running two years. They were issued at the critical period, when the war was unsettling the finances of both State and Nation. The State received $12,400, and returned $37,200 or 300 per cent. as principal and interest. This was a heavy penalty for poor credit.

High interest rates and heavy discounts combined to make the State's financial burdens especially heavy during this period of beginnings. As we find the highest State tax levy in 1869 (10 mills), so also do we find the per capita debt at its maximum at this identical time. Population and debt gradually increased during this period, causing fluctuations as follows:

STATE DEBT PER CAPITA, 1861–69

1861	$1.30
1862	1.27
1863	2.14
1864	3.50

1865 .... 3.35
1866 .... 3.32
1867 .... 3.44
1868 .... 3.65
1869 .... 3.95

Expenditure.—The expenditures of the State its first year were limited to its narrowest and most necessary functions, namely, to items of administration, the judiciary, education, legislation, and police, including defense and penal institutions. The penal expenses were those incurred in keeping State prisoners in county jails, pending the erection of a State Penitentiary. In the succeeding years, prior to 1870, new expenditure accounts were added to the budget in the following order: 1862, a State Library and Public Charities first come in for a share of the public funds; 1864, an Immigration Board is created, looking to the development of the State's material resources; 1867, an Agricultural Society is formed to further agriculture in the State; 1869, a Horticultural Society is created, and relief is granted to frontier settlers.

As compared with later years, the outlay for the year 1861 was extremely small and insignificant. The treasurer did not even publish a statement of the transactions of his office, and not till 1885, after a careful investigation of all the records was such a report issued. By this we find that warrants were issued to the amount of $62,613.33.

The principal items of the debt, as we saw by the bond issues above were public buildings, $615,500, and military expenses, $377,000.

For educational purposes there was a bond issue of $5,500 to help establish a State Agricultural College. But this does not indicate that the state outlay for education was low, but only that this outlay was made in some other way than through the aid of bond issue. For example, the very first legislature made an annual assessment and levy of a one-mill tax on the property of the State for the support of the common schools.[5] This was, in effect, an appropriation for a longer term than

---

[5] *Laws of 1861*, ch. 76, Sec. 5.

the constitution contemplated, but it went unchallenged for several years. The law was re-enacted in the General Statutes of 1868, and again in 1876, but was repealed in 1879.[6] The repeal was on constitutional grounds and was therefore sustained by the Supreme Court of the State.

In the matter of public buildings the State Agricultural College and the State University were the first to claim the State's attention, and in a manner explained below. A penal institution came in next for the State's attention, and the cost of this was distributed over a long period of years by a bond issue. The same policy was applied to the later buildings, the capitol being next in order. Pending the erection of this structure the legislature occupied rented quarters in the capital city. Outlay for public charity work was begun with the erection of the Deaf and Dumb Asylum at Olathe, followed with the Insane Asylum at Topeka.

Fiscal Administration.—The public school lands granted by the federal government constituted a magnificent domain. The State chose the policy of selling these lands rather than renting them on long-term leases. By this plan, it was thought, permanent improvements would be encouraged, and a more general development of the State's resources would follow.

A piece of costly folly was committed with the 500,000-acre domain, granted by Congress under the Act of 1841. This had been set aside by the Kansas Constitution as part of the common school permanent fund, but was perverted to another use by the legislature of 1866. After long wrangling in both Houses, it was voted to sell these lands and appropriate the proceeds to four railroad companies. Members of the minority opposed the bill as unconstitutional and put through by local personal interests.[7] The proceeds of this sale gave rise to a small railroad fund which was carried on the treasurer's books for many years. The amount due each road was so small that it was never called for by some of the roads, and was later put into the general revenue fund. Thus the proceeds of the

---

[6] *Genl. Stat. 1868*, ch. 92, Sec. 76.
[7] *Senate Journal*, Jan. 26, 1866. *House Journal*, Feb. 17, 1866.

500,000 acres were completely dissipated, the State realizing a minimum of gain at a maximum of cost.

Foundations for higher education were provided in the Act of Admission, and hence there was no period in her statehood when Kansas did not make this subject a matter of attention. Denominational colleges had already made beginnings, both at Manhattan, later the seat of the Agricultural College, and at Lawrence, destined to be the seat of the State University. The State acquired both of these small plants.

For a State University, there was a federal land grant of 46,080 acres. The citizens of Lawrence gave the State a bonus of $15,000 to secure the location of the University there. This was adequate to finance the young institution a few years, so far as buildings and apparatus were concerned, till its needs had expanded.

The State Normal School was founded at Emporia by the national grant of salt lands, aggregating 30,380 acres.

The Morrill Act of Congress, 1862, provided for the State Agricultural College. This Act gave Kansas 90,000 acres as a foundation for her agricultural school, an endowment much more valuable than that for her University or Normal School.

Management of state funds during this period shows some interesting developments. The administration of the school funds was placed by the constitution in the care of a commission of three men—the state superintendent of public instruction, the secretary of state, and the attorney general. By a law of 1861, they were empowered to lend these funds to the State of Kansas, or to citizens of Kansas, on real estate mortgage security. The custom became established, however, of investing these funds in the bonds of the State and the local divisions.

Up to the year 1868, not one cent had been levied and set apart for a sinking fund. Previous to 1867, the general revenue and interest funds were kept together under the heading of "revenue," and receipted for as "State tax." In the year 1867, these funds were separated, after a fashion, and entered under the two headings, revenue and sinking fund. But the accruing interest on the bonds amounted to so much that there was nothing left for a sinking fund. During the fiscal year of

1869, for the first time, the interest fund and the sinking fund were kept separate, and so remained. The sinking fund this year amounted to $29,715. Of this amount, $26,000 was borrowed by a joint resolution, and applied to the payment of State warrants. The idea of an inviolable sinking fund developed very slowly. This was partly due to the fact that interest on bonds regularly fell due January 1st, and State taxes not till January 10th, and hence it was necessary to make temporary loans on interest to meet this accrued bond interest, or else borrow from the available moneys in the sinking fund or some other fund. This led to the practice of transferring from one fund to another as emergencies arose. The number of funds greatly increased from year to year till their unwieldiness compelled a reform.

Appropriations during this period were quite regularly in excess of income. Many auditor's warrants were presented to the treasurer and stamped "unpaid for want of funds." The large amount of State scrip thus made during several successive years without making adequate provision for its payment, depreciated so much upon the market as to occasion serious loss to the State, and to create general complaint and dissatisfaction among the people.[8] These warrants bore interest at the rate of 7 per cent. from date of presentation till final payment. How general this practice was of stamping warrants unpaid, we know by the amount of interest paid yearly by the State on them. This is shown in the accompanying table:

INTEREST PAID ON STATE WARRANTS, 1861-69[9]

1861	$2,335 00
1862	9,031 84
1863	4,673 87
1864	4,219 95
1865	3,204 67
1866	2,331 19
1867	2,115 20

[8] *Treasurer's Report,* 1870·
[9] *Auditor's Report,* 1873.

1868 .... 4,676 80
1869 .... 9,098 79

          Total $41,687 31

Besides this scrip, there was another kind of floating debt which might be called "auditor-made scrip." The laws of 1868 authorized the auditor to issue certificates of indebtedness to meet all proper bills, not covered by legislative appropriation. These acts of the auditor were ratified by the legislature, and some $12,000 thus issued during the next two years.

There was much dissatisfaction at this time with the treasury machinery and its general management. An elaborate act was passed in 1866 whereby it was purposed to keep securely in special vaults and safes in the Treasury itself all the public money and to separate it entirely from commercial use. For the same thing was happening to treasurers here as had happened in other States, namely, they had embraced the opportunity of making private use of the public funds. If an extensive system of accounts, multiplied entries, numerous checks and guards, and frequent examinations of the treasury could have prevented this abuse of a public trust, this act would have succeeded. Under it each transaction was transcribed at least six times. As often as once a month and without previous notice or intimation it was made the duty of the governor, secretary and auditor, to make a thorough and complete examination of all vouchers, books and effects which belonged to the treasury, and to compare the same with the auditor's accounts, that there might be no deficiency. It was furthermore made a high crime, punishable by fine and imprisonment, to use, loan or deposit with banks or individuals any portion of the public moneys (except to pay interest on State bonds when it became due).

This act was never carried out. It was a practical impossibility to make the monthly examinations called for. Precedent had established the custom of using a Topeka bank for making collections and remittances, and this practice was continued. Neither were the public funds well safe-guarded, as later investigation showed.

A few more strictures were created by an act the succeeding year, the title of which explained its purpose to be "to restrain state and county officials from speculating in their office." Treasurers evidently did not believe in letting the public funds lie idle, even if the law did require it.

Claims.—As an aftermath of the war, a vast amount of claims were brought forward against the State. These came chiefly from the two important border raids,—the Quantrell Raid in 1863, in which Lawrence was sacked and looted, and the Price Raid in 1864. Since these were not warfare in the ordinary sense of the word,—there being no opposing forces,—those on whom suffering and losses were entailed brought demands against the State for payment. After repeated examinations of these claims, the legislaure in 1865 agreed to assume the Price Raid claims, looking to the general government for ultimate reimbursement. Action was taken by the government a few years later and these claims finally settled, as explained in a subsequent chapter.

The Quantrell Raid claims, however, dragged on for over thirty years. The legislature of 1901 made a satisfactory adjustment.

Railroads.—This was a period of beginnings in railroads and their development cannot be dissociated from the development of the State. Legislators' speeches and governors' messages referred to these roads in terms of unqualified optimism. "I call your special attention," says Governor Carney in 1863, "to the Pacific Railroad. No mightier work was ever undertaken by any government. It will put the Atlantic and Pacific in close neighborhood, and melt down, as it were, the Rocky Mountains, the only barrier the fathers feared could ever divide the Republic." Others thought that "these grand enterprises" would make Kansas the "great highway for the commerce of the world."[10] Perhaps the climax of optimism was reached in Governor Harvey's message of 1870, where he says, concerning the new railroad bridge across the Missouri river at Leavenworth; "It is being made a structure consonant with

---

[10] *Message of Gov. Crawford, 1866; Message of Gov. Harvey, 1869.*

the richness and beauty of its surroundings, and of utility equal to the demands which bid fair to make Kansas the highway of the continent, Leavenworth city the commercial emporium of the Missouri valley, and Fort Leavenworth the future capital of the United States.''

It is very plain, that had the constitution not expressly forbidden it, the State would have been a party in many railroad enterprises. Governor Carney (1863) spoke of a ''general State system of railroads.'' Governor Harvey (1869) used these words in speaking of recommended legislation: ''You should encourage in every judicious and proper manner the rapid construction of all these roads.''

These utterances revealed the true spirit of eagerness among the people to vote subsidies to these roads, an eagerness which could not be held in check, although the federal government was now granting these roads millions of acres of land. The State perverted from its original use the 500,000 acres of school land mentioned above, and dribbled its proceeds out from year to year among the railroads. But the constitutional check was sufficient to stop any further state activity in this direction. But a way was found around the constitutional barrier, since the people were determined to have the roads, and were satisfied that the best policy was one of direct aid. Hence came the law of 1865, authorizing counties to subscribe for stock in and issue bonds to railroad companies, to the extent of $300.000 to each county. The law soon came before the courts for construction. Leavenworth county had promptly voted aid to the Union Pacific to the amount of $250,000. The first bonds falling due in 1867, payment was refused. The courts upheld the validity of the bonds and construed the law as constitutional and binding.[11]

One important phase of the question of taxation of railroads was settled in connection with the Union Pacific in Kansas.[12] Congress had, in 1862, granted to this road a munificent land subsidy. The company was to receive every alternate section of land (odd numbers)) for ten miles on each side of the track,

---

[11] *Leavenworth county vs. Miller*, 7 *Kas.*, 479. *State vs. Nemaha county*, 7 *Kas.*, 542.
[12] *Report Texas Tax Commission*. 1899, p. 54 *seq.*

where such lands had not been sold or otherwise disposed of.[13] This amounted to about two and one-half million acres. Congress was importuned for more. Two years later an amendatory act was passed, authorizing the issue of first-mortgage bonds, and extending the above grant to twenty miles on each side of the road.[14] This made the grant about five million acres. The first-mortgage bonds in favor of the United States were later changed to second-mortgage bonds. In 1855 the territorial legislature of Kansas had chartered the Leavenworth, Pawnee & Western Railroad Company, and in 1862 the State legislature changed its name to the Union Pacific Railroad Company, Eastern Division, and authorized it to consolidate with any other company or companies, organized or to be organized under the laws of the United States, or of any State or Territory. Congress afterwards chartered the Union Pacific company. But the Eastern Division remained a State road, although Congress had subsidized it so liberally. It was assessed for State taxation. An injunction was asked and obtained, restraining the collection of the tax, upon the ground that the United States held a mortgage against the road, and that it was bound to perform certain duties, and ultimately to pay 5 per cent. of its net earnings to the United States, on which grounds, notwithstanding it was a State corporation having federal aid, it claimed exemption from taxation. The question was brought before the United States Supreme Court, where a decision was given in favor of Kansas. Chief Justice Chase rendering the opinion of the Court, held:[15]

"No one questions that the power to tax all property, business and persons, within their respective limits, is original in the States, and has never been surrendered. It cannot be so used, indeed, as to defeat or hinder the operations of the national government, but it will be safe to conclude in general, in reference to persons and State corporations employed in government service, that when Congress has not interposed to protect their property from State taxation, such taxation is not obnoxious to

---

[13] 12 *Statutes at Large*, 489.
[14] 13 *Statutes at Large*, 356.
[15] 76 *U. S.*, 579.

that objection. (*Lane county v. Oregon.* [*ante* 105]; *Bank v. Kentucky.* [*ante* 701]).

"We perceive no limits to the principle of exemptions which the complainants seek to establish. It would remove from the reach of State taxation all property of every agent of the government. Every corporation engaged in the transportation of mails or of government property of any description, by land or water, or in supplying materials for the use of the government, or in performing any service of whatever kind, might claim the benefit of the exemption. The amount of property now held by such corporations, and having relations more or less direct to the national government and its services, is very great. And this amount is continually increasing; so that it may admit of question whether the whole income of the property which will remain liable to State taxation, if the principle contended for is admitted and applied in its fullest extent, may not ultimately be found inadequate to the support of the State governments.

"The nature of the claims to exemption which would be set up is well illustrated in the case before us. The very ground of the claim is in the bounties of the general government. The allegation is, that the government has advanced large sums to aid in the construction of the road; has contented itself with the security of a second-mortgage; has made large grants of land upon no condition of benefit to itself, except that the company will perform certain services for full compensation, independently of those grants; and will admit the government to a very limited and wholly contingent interest in remote net income."

This settled the point that the State might tax a road having a federal charter. But the question was still open as to the taxation of federal land grants. The Amendatory Act of 1864[16] provided that "before any land granted in this act shall be conveyed to the said company * * * there shall first be paid into the treasury of the United States the cost of surveying, selecting, and conveying the same by the said company or party in interest, as the titles shall be required by said company." This reserved an equity in the United States, which the Supreme Court decided

---

[16] 13 *Statutes at Large*, 356, Sec. 21.

the State could not defeat or embarrass.[17]   In this way the railroads escaped taxation on all their congressional grants till such
lands were actually patented.   They were not patented, therefore much in advance of their sale, and in fact are not yet all
patented.   Taxes were also escaped in unorganized counties, and
this also relieved the railroads of thousands of dollars of taxation annually for many years.

Banking.—Provision was made by the legislature of 1861 for
the organization of banks of issue, with a minimum capital of
$25,000.[18]   This system, of course, did not have time to develop
to any great extent before the National Banking system was introduced by the federal government, driving out of circulation
the notes of State banks by the 10 per cent. tax. Specie payment
was not successfully maintained for a single year by the State
banks, for we find an act by the first legislature authorizing the
suspension of specie payment.[19]

[17] *Railway company v. Prescott,* 16 *Wallace,* 103.   *Railway company v. Mc-
Shane,* 22 *Wallace,* 444.
[18] *Laws of 1861,* ch. 4.
[19] *Laws of 1861, p.* 279.

CHAPTER V

PROSPERITY AND REACTION, 1869–1879

A few general features of this period must be noted before taking up the discussion of its financial history in detail. When the readjustment was made after the Civil War, a brief era of prosperity dawned for Kansas. Plenty of money was being spent,—borrowed money to be sure, but the time for repayment was far in the future. In the early seventies crops were good, and prosperity in agriculture meant prosperity for the whole state. The various state buildings were in process of erection and were a source of great local pride. Speaking of the new State University building, just finished at a cost of $138,500, the governor proudly said: "This structure is believed to be the best college building which has ever been erected in our country."[1] But the rejoicings of prosperity were soon turned into the wailings of calamity. The year 1874 was a memorable one in the annals of Kansas, being known as the Grasshopper year. It was at this time that the grasshoppers literally devastated the fields of the state. Destitution was so great that a special session of the legislature was called to devise means of relief. Authority was granted to counties to issue relief bonds, and the state issued bonds to purchase these. This was, of course, for the frontier regions, where the accumulated wealth was very meager indeed. The eastern part of the state was able to care for itself.

That peculiar social upheaval among the farmers, the Grange movement, gathered weight and strength with each fresh cause of discontent. The dramatic bribery case of United States Senator Pomeroy and a member of the legislature in 1873 was only

---

[1] *Message of Gov. Osborn,* 1873.

the beginning of a series of political peculations. The next year impeachment proceedings were instituted against the state treasurer, Josiah E. Hayes, for "high crimes and misdemeanors in office." His resignation put a stop to the proceedings. The year following, it developed that the school fund had been defrauded of a large amount through the connivance of Treasurer Lappin. He, too, resigned, but the matter was not dropped till loss to the State had been made good.

Tax Laws.—This was an interesting period in the state's history from the standpoint of her tax legislation and general fiscal affairs.

Dissatisfaction with the tax laws was becoming more general, and especially among the Grangers, who now began to give expression to their common feelings. They felt keenly the injustice of the prevailing assessment of personal property below its true value, or the entire escape of this property from taxation in many cases. They secured a law providing that assessors should meet and agree upon an "equal basis of valuation."[2] But the remedy proved worse than the disease, as subsequent developments will show. The matter of mortgage taxation was as little understood as the other phases of the subject. By some peculiar impulse, the legislature of 1873 enacted a law exempting mortgages from taxation, the purpose of the act, as expressed in its title, being "to promote the improvement of real estate by exempting mortgages and other securities from taxation."[3] With the farmers, the law had an immediate and overwhelming unpopularity. At their state convention in Topeka the same year they passed resolutions asking for its speedy repeal. The next legislature heeded the request and promptly repealed the law.[4]

Interest in tax affairs waxed sufficiently strong to demand the creation of a special tax commission in 1872, which gave a report the next year. But no important and permanent changes were made till the complete new tax law of 1876. This is an elaborate act, comprising twenty articles, and repealing practically all the tax laws before it. It was an attempt to correct in-

---

[2] *Laws of Kansas,* 1870. Chapter on Taxation.
[3] *Laws of Kansas,* 1873, ch. 140.
[4] *Laws of Kansas,* 1874, ch. 130.

equalities, and especially to reach personal property. Additional duties were imposed on assessors, and more stringent regulations on persons making returns.

Among its more important provisions we may note the following: Bona fide debts were to be subtracted from credits; all property was to be valued at its true value in money; banks were to continue the practice of paying the tax on all the shares of the stockholders (minus their real estate taxed locally); railroads were to be assessed by a state board, and the auditor was to levy the tax in unorganized counties; real estate, including all improvements, was to be assessed every two years from an actual view taken by the assessor; personal property was to be assessed annually, and, as before, the assessors were to meet and agree upon an equal basis of valuation.

The immediate effect of this act made it appear a success, for it seemed to be fulfilling its purpose admirably. The assessment of personal property was raised at once from $19,400,000 to $23,000,000, an increase of 18 per cent. in one year. The railroad assessment was raised from $12,000,000 to $16,000,000, an increase of 33 1-3 per cent. This relatively high assessment of personalty held out for eight years then the proportion of this kind of property rapidly declined in the assessment rolls for thirteen years. (See Appendix A.) The particulars of railroad taxation are detailed below, under the paragraph on railroads.

That the entire law of 1876 was not a successful piece of work, we can judge from the fact that at the next session of the legislature, only one year later, one article of the law was repealed entirely, and four amendments were added. Attacks were all directed at the law, and not at the system itself.

It was in the year 1879 when the legislature discontinued the levy of a direct state tax for common school purposes. This was accomplished by the repeal of the "one-mill levy law 1861."[5] Thereafter the income of the annual school fund was derived principally from interest upon the invested permanent school fund. Local taxation, it must be borne in mind, produced the

---

[5] *Laws of Kansas*, 1861, ch. 76, Sec. 5. "There is hereby levied and assessed annually one mill on the dollar for the support of the common schools of the State."

bulk of the income supporting the common school system. The one-mill levy was about equivalent to one month's wages for every teacher.

Income.—The state income during this period was not deranged by any wars or very serious disturbances of any kind. Direct tax furnished over 99 per cent. of the state's revenue. There were but slight fluctuations in the rate of the levy, and only a little variation in the total assessed valuations. The principal change occurred in the year 1876, under the stringent new law described above. This tax rate was lowered, but the revenue produced was greater than that of the year before. Particulars for each year can be seen in the short table below:

TOTAL ASSESSED VALUATIONS, LEVY AND RATE OF STATE TAXES,
1870–1879.

Year.	Assessed valuation.	State levy.	Rate in mills.
1870................................	$92,528,100	$809,621	8¾
1871................................	108,753.575	652,521	6
1872................................	127,690,937	1,085,373	8½
1873	125,684,177	754,105	6
1874................................	128,906,520	773,439	6
1875................................	121,544.344	729.266	6
1876................................	133,832.316	736,078	5½
1877	137.480,530	756.138	5½
1878..............................	138,698,811	762,843	5½
1879................................	144,930,280	942.046	6½

Fees, principally from insurance companies, began to form an item of income to the state at this time. They ranged from $10,000 to $15,000 a year. The tendency was plainly towards increasing this source of revenue. Within a few years, as we shall see, the number of fees was greatly multiplied, until they became of real fiscal significance.

Extraordinary revenue was only needed for two purposes; one, as mentioned before, relief for frontier settlers suffering from grasshopper devastations, and the other, defence against Indian raids along the southwestern border. For these two purposes, bonds were issued, and on terms showing that the credit of the state was at last sound. Considering the eastern money market, however, the rate of interest was rather high. Full particulars of these bond sales are exhibited in tabular form below:

BOND STATEMENT, 1870–1879.

Issued under act of	Date of issue.	Purpose.	Rate of interest	When due.	Face of bonds.	Amount sold for.
Oct. 15, '74	Oct. 15, '74	Relief.	7	Oct. 15, '94	$5,000	$5,000
Oct. 15, '74	Oct. 15, '74	" "	7	Oct. 15, '94	7,000	7,000
Oct. 15, '74	Oct. 15, '74	" "	7	Oct. 15, '94	500	500
Mar. 6, '75	Mar. 15, '75	Military.	7	Mar. 15, '95	36,500	36.500
Totals...					$49,000	$49,000

Thus we see that only $49,000 of income during this whole period was derived from the sale of bonds. The preeminence in bond issues now passes from the state to the municipalities.

Expenditure.—In the matter of expenditures for this decade we see a further expansion of the budget. Outlay along old lines increased, and new subjects of expenditure were introduced. In 1870 the state entered the domain of private charity, granting a subsidy of $10,000 to a purely private institution. This was the entering wedge. Soon the list of private charities receiving state aid had multiplied many fold. For the supervision of insurance, a state department of insurance was next established. Then for collecting and preserving historical matter pertaining to the state, an Historical Society was organized. In 1878 a Fish Commission appears for the first time. The first step taken to establish a purely state industry was in 1879, when we find an appropriation made for a coal mine at the state penitentiary. Other industries were developed later at this institution. On the subject of immigration the legislature had grown apathetic. Governors, however, urged the matter on their attention, and requested that they would at least issue pamphlets in English, German, and Scandinavian, for the purpose of drawing a desirable class of settlers to the vast prairies of the state. This work passed into the hands of the Board of Agriculture, where it was well taken care of, and the separate Board of Immigration ceased to exist.

Fiscal Affairs.—In the management of fiscal affairs during this period, the treasurer was not embarrassed with a deficit so frequently as had happened before. For in the preceding period it had been necessary every year to tide over the deficit by stamping warrants unpaid. During the first four years of this period interest on such warrants was paid by the treasurer to the amount of $51,414.[6]   And then, for the first time, the treasurer was able to pay all warrants as presented, and this condition held good for many years.

State bonds to the amount of $209,500 fell due this period and were promptly paid. $204,000 was in 7 per cent. bonds, and $5,500 in 10 per cent. bonds. This lessened the state's annual burden of interest by $14,830.

The sinking fund proved a source of contention and controversy till a satisfactory adjustment was made by the law of 1875. A serious attempt was made to violate this fund in the year 1870. A joint resolution was adopted, to appropriate a portion of the sinking fund to the payment of "current legislative expenses and the salaries of Supreme and District court judges." The governor vetoed the act as an unwarranted assumption of authority, since it created a "favored class of creditors of the State to the detriment of those with whom the people in their sovereign capacity, have made a sacred contract." He showed this to be in violation of the constitutional provisions, that the legislature shall provide each year for raising revenue sufficient to defray the current expenses of the state,[7] and that the proceeds from no tax shall be applied to any other purpose than that for which the tax was levied. He referred to the effect on public creditors and taxpayers. His veto was, however, overruled by a two-thirds majority in each House. The alternative of the members was to take their pay in the depreciated scrip of the state, or make an "unwarranted attack on the sinking fund." They chose the latter. An injunction was issued against the payment of the members from this fund, and a revenue bill passed to provide for the fiscal year 1870-71. This bill provided for the redemption of the state scrip which had depreciated in value and become an injury to the public credit.

The investment of the sinking fund, up to the year 1875, was

---

[6] *Auditor's Report,* 1873.

[7] This was the constitutional provis on till amended, Nov. 2. 1875. Provision was then made for revenue sufficient for two years. Following this change, in the year 1877, the sessions of the legislature became biennial instead of annual.

under the confusing and conflicting provisons of twenty-one separate acts. No particular person was made responsible for its investment, nor was any clear method of investment established. "The result," says the vigorous auditor of 1874, " is what might have been expected from such vague, loose and shabby legislation. The fund invests itself, as it sees fit, in its own good time, and in such manner and amounts as are convenient."

The 1875 law created a board of three commissioners (governor, auditor and secretary of state) to invest this fund, either in Kansas bonds, or United States bonds.[8] This removed all ambiguities from the law, and ensured a proper administration of this fund.

The permanent school fund proved a hard one to manage successfully, although it had been left with a commission from the beginning. Wisely or unwisely, a law was passed enlarging the powers of the commission by authorizing the investment of this fund in school district bonds. This had two evil results. Many bogus and fraudulent bonds were sold by rogues to the treasurer, and thus the school fund was defrauded of a large amount of money. Since the treasurer was a party to the fraud, the state was fully reimbursed later, for ample safeguards had been provided against a defalcating treasurer. The second evil was the over-issue of school district bonds which was thereby encouraged. We see this illustrated in many counties, one of which we may take as typical, namely, Sumner county in the south-central part of the state. A local paper here describes the situation in this language: "The school tax in district number 11 is 4.5 per cent., making over $20 per quarter-section [160 acres], just for school purposes. One quarter has $23.40 school tax, which with State, county and township added, runs it up to between $35 and $40. No quarter in district 22 has less than $22 school tax. One quarter in district 25 has $32.04 school tax; all the remaining taxes on it are only $11.05, making $43.09 on a single quarter-section. The district has $1,500 of bonds and only six quarters of land taxable. The taxable personal property in this district is all owned by one man, and he has gone to Iowa."[9]

[8] *Laws of Kansas*, 1875, ch. 143.

[9] *Wellington* (Sumner county) *Press*, Oct. 8, 1874. Quoted in *Auditor's Report*, 1874, p. 41.

Examples of frauds and excesses soon called forth new laws on the subject of the administration of this fund. A law in 1876 provided that it should be invested only in United States or Kansas State bonds, but also interposed the requirement that the fund should in no case be diminished, that is, that no bonds should be bought above par. This barred out the purchase of federal bonds. And the amount of State bonds was too small to purchase the entire permanent school fund. So the difficulty remained to be solved by subsequent legislation. The size of this fund increased rapidly throughout this decade, being increased from four different sources;—the sale of school lands, the proceeds of escheated estates, 5 per cent. on the sale of all government lands in the state, and the fees of insurance companies registered in the state under the law of 1871.

Claims.—The matter of the Price Raid claims was successfully brought before Congress in 1871, by the state agent. The Kansas auditing committee had allowed some $500,000 on these claims, but Congress scaled the amount down to $337,000, and this amount was paid over to the state.[10] The treasurer disbursed it on claims in the order of their presentation, till it was exhausted.

Insurance.—The subject of insurance began to be of fiscal importance to the State in this period. As early as 1863 the governor of the state had called attention to the fact that all the insurance was by foreign companies, who therefore paid no taxes, having no property in the state. Tax them, he said.[11] Nothing, however, was done, and, seven years later, another governor reminded the legislature that the insurance business had become important in the state.[12] In the year 1871, the Insurance Department was created, and regulations adopted necessary for the safety of policy holders.[13] The young department had a hard

---

[10] Hazelrigg, *History of Kansas*, p. 164.

[11] *Inaugural Message of Gov. Carney,* 1863.

[12] *Message of Gov. Harvey,* 1870.

[13] *(First Annual Report, Supt. of Insurance.)* Fees charged Insurance Companies under 1871 Law.
   a. Filing and examining charter and issuing certificate..............$50.
      Filing and examining statement............................... 50.
   b. Benefit of School Fund.. 50.
   c. Each license issued to agents..................................... 2.

struggle to survive for the first few years. The pugilistic auditor of 1874 vigorously attacked it as "rotten from stem to gudgeon."[14] But it very creditably stood a searching investigation by a legislative committee, and finally established a conviction of its usefulness.

In 1876, 78 companies were doing business in the state, and paid fees that year to the amount of $12,788.96.[15]

Railroads.—Kansas railroads during the seventies experienced a period of rapid expansion, followed by a reaction. Municipal aid was lavishly bestowed during the early part of the period. The extent of these subsidies can be seen in the statement below:[16]

MUNICIPAL AID TO RAILROADS, 1870–1878.

1870	$1,189,000
1871	830,000
1872	950,000
1873	249,000
1874	358,000
1875	39,600
1876	61,900
1877 1878	646,000
Total	4,324,000

This was simply a phase of the railroad-building epidemic sweeping over the whole country. Only Kansas seemed to be the hot-bed of the disease. The process was ruinous to both the people and the roads, for the need of roads was oversupplied and many roads long remained non-dividend paying.

Much experimenting was done at this time with the methods of taxing the railroads of the state. An abortive attempt was made in 1871 to establish a State Board of Assessors as a permanent part of the tax machinery.[17] The law was good, but proved to be five years ahead of public opinion. Corruption was scented by the reformers of the state, and the cry went up that railroads were not paying their share of taxes under the State Board as-

[14] Auditor Wilder's *Report*, 1874; Governor Anthony's *Message*, 1877.
[15] *Message of Gov. Osborn*, 1876.
[16] Compiled from *First Ann. Report, Board of R. R. Commissioners*, p. 42-46, and *Auditors' Reports*, 1874 to 1878.
[17] *Laws of 1871*, ch. 150.

sessment. The law was repealed in 1874, and the old method of assessment by city and township assessors re-instated. A crude provision for ensuring equality was incorporated in the law in these words, "Such property shall be treated in all respects in regard to assessment and equalization the same as other property belonging to individuals, except that it shall be treated as property belonging to railroads, under the terms, 'land,' 'railroad track,' 'lots,' and 'personal property.'"

Returns made under this system of assessment very naturally show some queer cases of equality. Injustices between localities were aggravated prodigiously. County clerks' returns show cases like the following:[18] The Atchison, Topeka & Santa Fe was valued at $3,067 per mile in one county, and $6,254 in the next.[19] The Atchison and Nebraska railroad was assessed at $3,652 a mile in Atchison county, and at $10,384 in the adjoining county. It is unnecessary to multiply these illustrations. They show the fallacy of treating railroads as fractional bits of individual property scattered over the different counties. The law was elaborately amended the next year, but still leaving sworn statements to county clerks the basis of assessment. Gross and net income, earning capacity, etc., seem to have been treated by the law as playing an unimportant part in the road's ability to pay taxes. On the other hand, the law covers these points: Right-of-way, track, roadbed, ties, weight of iron or steel in tracks, what joints or chairs are used, ballasting (gravel or dirt), buildings on right-of-way, length of time iron in track has been used, rolling stock, capital stock (authorized and paid up), market value, "total listed valuation of all tangible property in the State." All these things, the law says, are to be considered as personal property. Then, as a sort of postscript to this law, franchises are mentioned, with the stipulation that they are to be listed and assessed with other personal property.

This law as amended survived but a single year. Then the tax law of 1876 took its place, as described on a preceding page. The State Board of Railroad Assessors was revived, and, now

---

[18] *Auditor's Report*, 1874.
[19] Reno and Sedgwick counties.

that the Grangers had made their demonstrations, room was not left for the criticism that the roads were assessed too low.

Municipal Finance.—The history of municipal finance during this period centers largely about one point, namely, the bond registery law of 1872.[20] There was a vague, general feeling over the state that new municipalities were getting heavily involved in their debts of different kinds, but there was as yet no social consciousness of the real magnitude of these obligations. It was deemed advisable, therefore, to provide by law for the registry of these bonds with the auditor of state, partly that the actual conditions might be known, and partly that the bonds might have a better standing with the money markets of the East. This was a comprehensive law, called by its critics a modern machine for making bonds at wholesale. By it, every local division was authorized to freight itself with debt beyond even the possibility of payment. The law provided for three things: The amount of bonds to be voted; their registry; and the manner of their payment. Bonds were permitted to the amount of 10 per cent. of the total taxable property of any municipality. This was the general rule. But each county could issue $100,000 in addition to the 10 per cent. limit, and if the county had an assessed valuation of $3,000,000 or over, it could issue $200,000 of bonds beyond the 10 per cent. limit. And each township, if it had *less* than $200,000 of taxable property, could vote aid to any railroad at the rate of $600 for every mile within the township. And as a final proviso, this act did not apply to any bonds previously voted, or vote then pending.

A concrete case will illustrate the import of this section of the law. Take Leavenworth county, for example. Its assessed valuation was $8,863,665, so that under the law it had a right: (1) to borrow (10 per cent. on valuation) $886,000; (2) to increase this debt by $200,000; and (3) any debt previously voted, not included (x).

Leavenworth county issued bonds to the limit. The population of the county was 32.444; the debt contracted, $1,100,000, or $200 per family.

---

[20] *Laws of 1872*, ch. 68.

As to the registry of these bonds—holders of the bonds were to present them to the state auditor for registration. "If the bonds are genuine," reads the statute, " he shall under his seal of office certify upon such bonds the fact that they have been regularly and legally issued, that the signatures thereto are genuine, and that such bonds have been registered at his office according to law."

This was imposing duties on the auditor which he had neither time nor inclination to fulfill.

Touching the payment of these bonds, we find the most striking provision of all. It was made the auditor's duty to assess each year the municipalities for an amount necessary to pay the accruing interest on their bonds, and to create a sinking fund for their final redemption. This sum was to go into the hands of the state treasurer, and to be by him disbursed in the payment of interest and principal when due. This made the bonds, virtually and in fact, as good securities as the state bonds themselves.

New York financiers, floating these bonds, exploited this law freely. They issued pamphlets proclaiming that they had for sale "Seven Per Cent. County Bonds: Registered by State Auditor: Interest and Principal paid by State Treasurer."[21] *The Commercial and Financial Chronicle* of New York, commended this law to the attention of capitalists.[22] "The passage of this law by the Legislature of Kansas," said the *Chronicle*, "was apparently a good policy, as it gives an additional assurance of security to the various issues of city, county and town bonds."

The law facilitated debt-making too much. It failed of popularity in Kansas. The Farmers' Convention in Topeka—the same that opposed the exemption of mortgages from taxation— drew up resolutions, affirming that "the practice of voting municipal bonds is pernicious in its effects, and will inevitably bring bankruptcy and ruin upon the people, and we are therefore opposed to all laws allowing the issuance of such bonds."

The state auditor was hostile to the law since he had no means of determining when bonds were "regularly and legally issued,"

---

[21] *Kans. Misc. Pamphlets,* vol. I, No. 15; in Wisconsin His. Soc. Library.
[22] Vol. xiv, p. 457. Apr. 6, 1872.

without making a personal investigation, nor could he know whether the signatures were genuine. Nor did he even like the greater security given to the bonds by his official seal, for, as Auditor Wilder tersely said, "Rogues know this." Swindles were soon perpetrated under the act. Fraudulent bonds were issued for three imaginary cities in Cherokee county, Gregory, Cloud and Budlong,—and these bonds were bought by a New York Banking House for $68,000. "We are acquainted with one transaction," says the New York *Commercial and Financial Chronicle* of this date, "when $100,000 of such bonds were cashed (not by an infant or an idot either), to find a few months later that the city issuing them never existed except on paper."[23]

The treasurer refused to obey this law. He disliked the provision for the payment of municipal interest and debt through the state treasury. Although the law was mandatory, he refused to open separate books for municipal bond business.

The law was soon modified to such an extent that it amounted almost to a repeal. The amount of indebtedness allowed was reduced from 10 per cent. to 5 per cent. of taxable property, except in cases of bridges and county poor houses, and the auditor was relieved of the duty of making the annual levy of taxes for interest and sinking fund. The registration feature, however, was very wisely left in force.

Opinion concerning municipal aid to railroads crystallized into two statutes in 1876.[24] A majority of two-thirds was sufficient to authorize a subsidy, and the limits set were for a county, $100,000 and 5 per cent. of the taxable property, and for a township or city, $15,000, and 5 per cent. of its taxable property; *provided however,* that in no case should the total aid granted exceed $4,000 a mile. This was a general law, but it is interesting to notice how frequently subsequent legislatures allowed special exemptions from its operations.

The voting of municipal aid to private industries was going on at a lively pace till a court decision in 1873 gave it a temporary set-back. For instance, in 1870 the city of Burlingame,

[23] May 6, 1876.
[24] *Laws of 1876*, chs. 106, 107.

Osage county, was authorized to vote $25,000 in bonds to aid in establishing a woolen mill in that city.[25]   In 1872, Smoky Hill township, Mc Pherson county, was authorized to aid in erecting a flouring mill and to vote $6,000 in 10 per cent. bonds.[26]   In 1873 we find both general and special laws of the same tenor. Counties of over 30,000 population are authorized to issue bonds to the amount of $41,000 to aid in the construction of starch works.[27]   An examination of the session laws of this year will show a record like this:

Rice county is authorized to issue $7,000 in bonds to "develop coal beds."[28]

Grasshopper Falls township is authorized to issue $20,000 in 10 per cent. 10-year bonds, to aid manufacturing enterprises.[29]

Parker township, Morris county: $10,000, 10 per cent., 15-year bonds, to aid coal and manufacturing company.[30]

Home township, Nemaha county: $25,000, 10 per cent., 5-year bonds, for prospecting for coal, oil and gas.[31]

Kentucky township. Jefferson county: $10,000, 7 per cent., 10-year bonds, to build a flour mill.[32]

Blue Rapids township, Marshall county: $10,000, 10 per cent., 10-year bonds, to aid a manufacturing establishment.[33]

Atchison county: $150,000 to aid a railroad.[34]

The important legal questions involved in these bond issues were brought before the Kansas Supreme Court in the case of the *Commercial National Bank Cleveland vs. the City of Iola*.[35] Here it was held:

(1) *Special Laws* are unconstitutional and void.

(2) *Private Enterprises*, taxation in aid of, is void.

(3) *Taxation: Object and Purposes*: Taxation is a mode of raising revenue for *public purposes*. When it is prostituted to

---

[25] *Laws of 1870*, ch. 36.
[26] *Laws of 1872*, ch. 85.
[27] *Laws of 1873*, ch. 33.
[28] *Ibid.*, *1873*, ch. 37.
[29] *Ibid.*, *1873*, ch. 39.
[30] *Ibid.*, *1873*, ch. 41.
[31] *Ibid.*, *1873*, ch. 44.
[32] *Laws of 1873*, ch. 48.
[33] *Laws of 1873*, ch. 51.
[34] *Laws of 1873*, ch. 52.
[35] 9 Kans, 689.

objects in no way connected with the public interests, it ceases to be taxation and becomes plunder; and the establishment of a bridge manufactory or foundry, owned by private individuals, is essentially a private enterprise.

(4) *Municipal Bonds: Want of Power to Issue, Notice of Presumed:* Bonds issued by a municipality in aid of strictly private enterprises, are void—void from the beginning, and void into whosesoever hands they may have come.

The state attorney, citing this decision, said all bonds of this description were void, and money collected from the people to pay them, was not taxation but robbery, and no officer should levy and no person should pay such a tax.[36]

One would naturally expect this decision to have a deep lasting effect upon the bond legislation in Kansas. But such was not the case. There was some latitude left for the interpretation of the phrase "private enterprise." Railroads, of course, did not come in this class. Many people considered flouring mills as being something more than private enterprises. The passage of special laws received but very little check indeed from this decision. So, on the whole, the effects of the decision were only temporary, although a period of debt repudiation was initiated by it.

Leavenworth county and city furnish one of the most conspiciuous cases of municipal debt repudiation of this period. Holders of bonds of these two municipalities brought a motion before the United States Circuit Court in 1878, against the officials of the above corporations to attack them for contempt for not making a tax levy to pay the judgment on the coupons of their bonds. The citizens of the county arose against the procedure and upheld their officials in disobeying the court. The debt of the county and city had run up to over $2,000,000, twice the state debt. A compromise, as was usual in these cases, was effected and the creditors had to be satisfied with the payment of the debt as thus scaled down.

An official report before a special session of the legislature in 1875 shows what excesses these municipalities of the state indulged in, and how inevitable compromise or bald repudiation

---

[36] *Auditor's Report*, 1873, p. 14, 15.

was.[37]   This was the period of reaction in the state, and this report before the legislature showed the following deplorable conditions:

(1) Harper county had but 641 inhabitants and a bonded debt of $40,000, or $62.40 per capita.

(2) Comanche county had only 634 inhabitants, and a bonded debt of $72,000, or $113.57 per capita.

(3) Barber county had but 608 inhabitants, and a bonded debt of $141,300, or $232.40 per capita.

Considering a family as consisting of five persons, Barber county found itself burdened with a hopeless debt of $1,162 per family.

And yet this was practically only the beginning of municipal debt-making in Kansas.   Where compromises were not attempted, the debt was usually refunded, and thus the burden of debt paying was put off some twenty years, that is, till in the nineties.   At that time the burden did not prove any lighter.

---

[37] *Laws of Kansas,* Special Session, 1875, ch. 2.

CHAPTER VI

CRAZE IN RAILROAD EXPANSION, 1879–1889

This was a decade of expansion in Kansas. The reaction of '74 had been forgotten. Railroad building was pushed with unheard-of rapidity, over 6,000 miles of new line being constructed in ten years. Expansion grew into speculation, especially during the years 1883 to 1888. Eastern capital was lavishly loaned, not only to further the railroad enterprises, but also on mortgage security. The business of banking was practically unregulated by the state, and remained so till the passage of a banking law a few years later. This gave rise to an irregular system of banking, for many institutions that had originally been organized as real estate loan companies, and many individuals and firms were engaged in receiving deposits, while their principal business was entirely foreign to legitimate banking.[1] Many of these alleged banks had not only their entire capital, but a large portion of their deposits invested in unproductive and unsalable real estate.

Building and loan associations sprang into prominence during this period. First came the local associations of the small towns, usually organized for the sole purpose of assisting in building homes for persons of moderate means. Their boards of directors were as a rule composed of substantial business men, serving without pay. These were fruitful of much good. But these local institutions popularized the loan association business, and soon advantage was taken of this by bogus concerns, principally "national" building and loan associations. These began about 1880 to operate extensively in the state and were soon transacting millions of dollars' worth of business,

---

[1] 2 *Bien. Report, Bank Comm.*, 1893-94.

largely with eastern capital. The state furnished no official supervision or scrutiny of these concerns, until the whole commonwealth was overrun with them. Many of these companies were "organized by men wholly unfitted by experience to conduct this business successfully, and others were organized, judging from their manner of transacting business, for the sole purpose of robbing their customers at both ends of the line. Companies with an alleged capital of $25,000, $50,000, or $100,000, with probably not more than 10 per cent. paid up, did not hesitate to guarantee the payment, both principal and interest, of loans amounting to millions of dollars, which were often disposed of through gross misrepresentations as to the value of the securities and the standing of the companies. When the time for the payment of these obligations arrived, troubles began."[2]

This was a period of speculation, as has been said. Irrigation was being pushed in the arid region of the state. This was the season of eastern speculation in real estate mortgages. For it was at this time that Kansas had the unenviable record of leading the whole United States in the per cent. of her mortgaged farms. Much over half of her farm land was mortgaged. If we may accept the returns of the Eleventh Census on this point in the years 1886, 1887, 1888, 1889 and 1890 the per cent. of mortgaged lands of the total farm land was 60.38, 68.92, 72.70, 70.29 and 60.32 per cent. respectively.[3] Only two other states, Nebraska and South Dakota, had over half their land mortgaged.

The question of the prohibition of the manufacture and sale of intoxicating drinks in Kansas came to a decision at this time. It was of course a social question of subsidiary fiscal importance in local finance. For many urged the argument that saloon license fees were necessary for the support of the city schools. But when the matter was put to the people, a constitutional

---

[2] 2 *Report Bank Comm.*
[3] *11th Census:* Volume on *Real Estate Mortgages.* The States nearest the Kansas record of 1890 were—

S. D...51.76 per cent.	Ia.....46.95 per cent.	N. Y...40.43 per cent.
Nebr...54.73 per cent.	D. C...51.25 per cent.	N. D...46.73 per cent.

amendment was adopted forever prohibiting the manufacture and sale of intoxicants in Kansas.[4]

Tax Laws.—The tax laws of this decade represent little change of any importance or wisdom. Each governor discussed the subject in his message to the legislature, urging revision of the laws. Such revision was needed, Governor Martin argued, because the laws' defects, universally recognized, were organic.[5] But the short biennial session of the legislature gave little time or opportunity for devising any new methods of taxation, or improving on the old. The stereotyped exhortation of "rigid economy," sounded in each gubernatorial message, together with the jealousy of the public over new expenditures influenced the legislature to refrain from incurring the expense of a tax commission of any kind. So the matter drifted on till sufficient grievances were accumulated to command popular attention. But it was over a decade after the close of this period when a tax commission is heard of again. The principal tax legislation at this time pertained to railroads and Pullman sleeping cars, and this will be explained under the discussion of railroads below.

Income.—The income of the state during this decade was sufficient to meet all current expenses, and was free from any violent fluctuations. As Governor St. John expressed it in 1881; "We are creating no new debts, but pay as we go." In fact there was regularly a surplus in the treasury of considerable magnitude, although the tax rate was lower than at any previous time. Since the tax laws remained uniform throughout the period, the total assessed valuations reflected the same uniformity, increasing gradually from year to year till 1889, when a maximum was reached. Then began a period of decline.

State treasurers reported assessed valuations and taxes as follows:

---

[4] Amendment adopted Nov. 2, 1880.
    Vote for......92,302= 52¼ per cent.
    Vote against...84,304= 47¾ per cent.
    Majority for.. 7,998= 4½ per cent.
[5] *Message of Gov. Martin,* 1889.

Year.	Assessed valuations.	State levy.	Rate in mills.
1880............................	$160,570,761	$883,139	$5\frac{1}{2}$
1881............................	170,813,373	854,066	5
1882............................	186,128,139	837,576	$4\frac{1}{2}$
1883............................	203,184,489	873,693	$4\frac{3}{10}$
1884............................	237,020,391	1,066,592	$4\frac{1}{2}$
1885............................	248,846,811	1,032,714	$4\frac{3}{20}$
1886............................	277,113,323	1,136,134	$4\frac{1}{10}$
1887............................	310,871,447	1,274,573	$4\frac{1}{10}$
1888............................	353,248,333	1,448,318	$4\frac{1}{10}$
1889............................	360,815,073	1,515,423	$4\frac{2}{10}$

Aside from taxation, the state derived a small income from
fees and from the industries conducted at the state penitentiary.
The principal fees were derived from insurance companies, aggregating from $15,000 to $20,000 a year.

Expenditures.—The expenditures of the state during this
period show a widening of the field of state activity, and the
gradual assumption of new powers and responsibilities. Both
the health of the citizens, and their material interests were made
matters of public concern and were, to a certain extent, taken
into the state's care. This we see in the creation of new "commissions," "boards," "bureaus," etc., and in certain other new
lines of expenditure. To give a mere catalogue of these addi-
tions to the state's economy during this decade, we have the following list: First, the railroad commission, to secure justice
in rates, charges, etc., as between the railroad corporations and
the individuals of the state; a mine inspector comes next; a live
stock sanitary commission is organized to safeguard the stock-
raising interests of the state, especially against incursions of
diseased Texas cattle; a labor bureau is now first heard from;
the state board of health is created in 1887; a silk commission
is also established the same year to transplant this exotic industry to Kansas soil; a wise provision is made at this time for a
forestry commission, for the state's needs along this line are beyond question. A sugar subsidy is granted in 1889 to foster the
culture of the sugar beet in Kansas, but this, like the silk com-

[68]

mission idea above, proves rather chimerical. The beef combine commission of 1889 completes the catalogue of new expenditures. for this period.

By an inspection of these functions, we see that some represent mere temporary activities; others permanent. Mine inspection and railway supervision, for instance, must by their very nature remain permanent state activities. Another function, discernible in the above list is that of protection, in the same sense as the federal protective tariff is said to be a protection to infant industries. Thus, the silk commission is obviously intended merely to put this young industry on its feet and then let it walk alone. So also the policy of granting subsidies to growers of sugar beets. We see this industrial side of the state developing from year to year. Had the state constitution not expressly forbidden the state's being a party to any works of internal improvement, we would doubtless have seen some extravagant operations in this field. For many times pressure was brought to bear on the legislature for direct and open aid from the state to private enterprises. A typical example is furnished by a case in 1885, when the sorghum sugar industry in the hands of a few private individuals gave promise of at least great possibilities. Their hope of state aid was strong enough to embolden them to seek it. The governor presented their wishes to the legislature in these words, "It is urged by a number of citizens, that the state should encourage this industry, and I call your attention to their suggestion."[8] But direct aid of this kind had to come from the municipalities.

Fiscal Affairs.—The chief item of interest in the fiscal affairs of this period is the public debt. A little over one-half million dollars of bonded debt fell due. Of this, $452,500 was bearing 7 per cent. interest; $101,275, 6 per cent. interest. This was all paid excepting $103,000, which was refunded at 4 per cent. by an issue of 20-year bonds. These were all purchased by the permanent school fund and hence the state simply had to pay interest to itself on them. The payment of these matured bonds meant a decrease of $33,631 in the state's annual interest expenditure.

[8] *Message of Gov. Martin, 1885.*

The sinking fund was wisely administered at this time, under the provisions of the 1875 law. United States bonds to the amount of $98,600 were purchased at a little above par. These were sold a little later at 119¼, thus realizing for the state a premium of $18,950.50.[7] Another large increase to this fund came from the payment of certain claims by the government. The sum of $332,308.13 was remitted for expenses incurred in "repelling invasions and suppressing Indian hostilities."[8] There was placed $282,500 to the credit of the sinking fund· and to the general revenue fund, $49,808.13.

The school fund was augmented considerably during this period by the sale of school lands. At first the state had been rather prodigal with these lands and loose in her methods of disposing of them, letting them go at under-appraised values. The idea of saving the unearned increment in these lands to the state failed to gain very much favor, and hence the policy of selling them as rapidly as possible was inaugurated. Their increase in value falling thus to the settlers, it was hoped, would stimulate permanent improvements and a more rapid development of the state's resources. Before certain regulations were interposed in 1886, these lands were frequently the subject of speculation in such manner as to defeat the state's aim of permanent improvements. According to the opinion of the state's attorney general, the permanent school fund, up to 1886, had lost at least $1,000,000 through lack of proper attention to the sale of school lands and through frauds perpetuated by syndicates, speculators, etc. "Before the passage of this act," says the attorney general,[9] "the practice has been for speculators to hire four young men or at least four individuals, equipped with a wagon and team of horses, cattle or mules, and four little houses made of lumber so arranged that they could be put together with bolts in a very short time. They would come to the center of a section of school land, each locating upon the inner corner of a quarter-section, and there remain for a day or two, until the easily beguiled appraisers appeared, when the lands would be appraised as having been settled upon and im-

---

[7] *Treasurer's Report*, 1883-84.
[8] *Special Message of Gov. Martin*, 1886.
[9] *5 Bien. Report, Att'y. Genl.*, 1885-86.

provements made to the extent of $25. The appraisers would disappear, and so would the settlers. The evening or the next morning would find them comfortably settled upon another section of school land, where during the following day they would again be visited by the appraisers, and in this manner they would move from section to section, and it is safe to say that thousands and thousands of acres of school lands have thus been fraudulently sold at $3 an acre, worth, in fact, from $3 to $10."

The most serious faults of this loose system were these

`(1) The control of the sale of school lands was in the hands of those who wanted to buy.

(2) Appraisement was made by immediate neighbors of those who wanted to buy.

(3) Proceeds of sales were reduced by big fees allowed local officers, amounting to from $12,000 to $16,000 annually. Defalcations of county treasurers also cost this fund some $40,000.

The creation of a state land department, under the 1886 act, gave this business the unified and central control which it needed.

Railroads.—This decade stands out above all others in Kansas history for its pre-eminence in railroad building. It has been variously described as a craze, a mania, and even a delirium in railway construction. The figures themselves are an eloquent description of the situation and so they are presented. For convenience's sake, the table also shows the subsidies granted each year:

RAILWAY MILEAGE (MAIN TRACK) AND SUBSIDIES, 1879-89.

Year.	Total mileage.	Yearly increase.	Municipal subsidies.
1879	2,444	142 }	$1,067,540
1880	3,478	1,034 }	
1881	3,701	223 }	589,485
1882	3,786	85 }	
1883	3,870	84 }	239,500
1884	4,020	150 }	
1885	4,181	161 }	961,000
1886	4,522	341 }	
1887	6,212	1,690 }	8,544,550 50
1888	8,312	2,100 }	
1889	8,721	409	804,250 (including 1890.)
Totals	8,721	6,277	$12,206,325 50

These totals do not include the 142 miles of increase from 1878 to 1879, but only show the increase for one decade, which is 6,277 miles. The remarkable increase of 2,100 miles was made in the year 1888. This was as much as had been built during the first twenty-five years of the state's history. And in these first twenty-five years population had increased six-fold, or from 107,000 to 650,000. But during this decade of railroad expansion while the roads increased 257 per cent., population increased only 75 per cent. This shows that there was too much of a stimulus somewhere and a glance at the right-hand column in the above table will show where it was.

A change in public feelings towards railroads begins to show itself in this period. We no longer find them referred to proudly as "these grand enterprises." Instead, they are called a source of anxiety and apprehension.[10] The actual status of public opinion on the railroad question was summed up in a masterly manner in Governor Glick's message of 1883, and an extended quotation from this will be very much in point. He said, in part, "It is a recognized fact that the railroads have, in a sense, made the state. They have by means of circulars and pamphlets extensively advertised the state, and thus brought it to the attention of thousands of immigrants who have settled among us, and are now an important class of our population. They have aided in the general material development of our resources, and have proved themselves an invaluable agency; and all this is thoroughly appreciated by the public.

"While this is true, it is equally true that the state has made the railroads; so that a mutual obligation exists between them. To encourage and promote and aid the building of railroads throughout the state, our citizens very wisely procured from the General Government large grants of lands, supplemented by a donation from our own state of 500,000 acres of our school lands and government and municipal bonds with first-mortgage guaranteed bonds, amounting to about $27,806,000; so that millions of acres of land and millions of dollars of money have been donated to aid in the construction of the various railroads of the state.

---

[10] *Message of Gov. Martin,* 1885.

"These generous donations of lands and bonds were made by the people of Kansas for the purpose of building the magnificent railroad system of the state, and for their generous treatment they expected generous, or at least, fair treatment in return, and for years this expectation was fully met. These liberal subsidies at the outset, enabled the projectors of our railroads not only to build and equip and maintain the roads in question in a style second to none in the country, but they also placed the original constructors in a position to greatly enrich themselves as individuals. * * * And yet, profitable as railroad building has been to the construction companies, the state and the people did not complain or interpose any obstacles to the successful construction of railroads, until the passage of the 'consolidation act' [1870], authorizing railroads to consolidate and lease railroads. "

Advantage was taken of this act, says Governor Glick, and by methods of "pooling their earnings," "stifling competition," and other "high-handed and outrageous things," the roads did serious wrongs to the people. Another evil adverted to by the Governor was the manipulation of state politics by the railroads. He further complained that the roads were shifting their own burden of taxation on the Kansas farmer. "Never," concludes the Governor, "in the history of the world have any people been subjected to greater abuses than have the people of Kansas for the last five years."

This ringing philippic against the railroads called forth some legislative action on the subject. A state board of railroad commissioners was created. The law provided that this commission should be maintained by a *pro rata* tax on the railroads, according to their assessed valuation, but the Kansas Supreme Court denied the validity of such a law.[11] The powers of this commission were much restricted, being principally advisory. However, some results were accomplished in lowering freight rates, lessening discrimination, and curing local disaffections. Complaint was made that more power should be given to this board. This board, of course, had nothing to do with the assess-

---

[11] *First Report, Board of R. R. Commissioners,* 1883.

ment of railroads, that falling to the state board of railroad assessors.

Railroads put out collateral branches for the conquest of adjacent territory—"system perfecting" as they called it. Preliminary surveys were made through the numerous cities, towns, and villages, and very often just outside, or within a few miles of these places. This was to stir up emulation and rival bidding among the municipalities on or near the projected road. For it generally happened that the settlers were already convinced that this prospective road was the one thing wanting to their permanent prosperity. And indeed, today many towns illustrate the force of this railroad factor in making or marring a place, for, scattered over the prairies of the state are numerous towns that, as soon as a railroad came to them, sprang ahead of their neighbors that got no roads. But towns were not satisfied with one road. They were just as anxious to secure a second, and thus become junction points. And in view of these facts, we can understand why such enormous aid was granted by the municipalities.

According to the *Fourth Annual Report of the Board of Railroad Commissioners*, the municipalities, up to the year 1884, had voted railroad bonds amounting to $9,504,385.50. From July 1, 1885, to November 1, 1886—that is, one year and four months, they voted $10,151,600. While some of these bonds were never issued, still the amount sold was vast, compared with the wealth of the communities issuing them.

The question may be asked, how could such enormous subsidies be granted under the limitations of the 1876 law? This was a general law, as we saw, limiting county aid to $100,000, plus 5 per cent. of the taxable property of the county, and with the general proviso that the total amount of aid should not exceed $4,000 a mile to any railroad.[12] If we examine subsequent legislation, we find repeated instances of special laws exempting municipalities from the operation of this general law.

Mission Township in Neosho county, for example, was permitted to aid Kansas railroad companies to the amount of $25,000, and was authorized to grant $4,000 a mile to "any rail-

---

[12] *Laws of 1876*, chs. 106, 107.

road that may be hereafter constructed through said township.''
A specific exemption was granted from the limitations of the
1876 law.[13] Another statute authorized certain townships to vote
aid to an amount so that a levy of 1 per cent. would pay the
interest on the bonds, and were at the same time made exempt
from the 1876 limitations.[14] Still another township, the same
year, was allowed to vote aid to the extent of $25,000.[15]

The legislature of 1887 passed another general law, limiting
total aid to railroads to $2,000 a mile.[16] This was, of course, after
the mischief had largely been done. The pressure of public opinion was strong enough so that a strict observance of this law
might have been expected. But the same legislature that enacted
this law passed four other laws tending to weaken it or con-
travene it directly.

A bond issue of the city of Lyons of $35,000 was legalized.[17]
The city of Winfield was authorized to vote $50,000 of railroad
aid.[18] Ellsworth township had illegally voted $40,000 in Sep-
tember, 1886, and this action was now legalized.[19] Likewise
the action of Cawker township under a previous law, was legalized.[20]

Many of these bonds were for 30 years at 10 per cent., so that
for each dollar received the municipality ultimately returned
four dollars. Six per cent. was the lowest rate of interest, but
higher rates were the most common.

A great deal of litigation was had as to the legality of these
bonds, but the almost invariable result was that the courts af-
firmed the binding nature of these obligations.[21]

This aid of the municipalities was in addition to the magnificent land subsidies donated by the general government and by
the state. The extent of these land gifts is exhibited in the following table:

---

[12] *Laws of 1886*, ch. 132.
[14] *Laws of 1886*, ch. 136.
[15] *Laws of 1886*, ch. 137.
[16] *Laws of 1887*, ch. 183.
[17] *Laws of 1887*, ch. 187.
[18] *Ibid., 1887*, ch. 189.
[19] *Ibid., 1887*, ch. 193.
[20] *Ibid.*, ch. 194.
[21] *Fourth Ann. Report, R. R. Commissioners*, p. 4, 5.

RAILROAD LAND GRANTS IN KANSAS.[22]

Union Pacific (Kansas Division)	5,087,123 55 acres
Atchison, Topeka and Santa Fé	2,930,338 00 acres
Missouri, Kansas and Texas	1,041,769 17 acres
Kansas City, Lawrence and Southern Kansas	245,574 00 acres
Kansas City, Fort Scott and Gulf	89,672 43 acres
Total	9,394,477 15 acres

Counting this land worth $3.50 per acre—a very low average— we get a total value of $32,880,670 for these land gifts to the five railroads.

Taxation was escaped on nearly all this land, by the simple method of not perfecting the title on it till it was needed for purposes of sale. Thus the Union Pacific, up to January, 1882, had only taken out patents on 883,772 acres, leaving several millions in its own hands for all purposes except taxation. This represented a loss to the state of some $250,000 in taxes annually. Here then was a plain case where the unearned increment went to the holders of the land.

A provision appears in the Compiled Laws of 1885, requiring the roads in unorganized counties to pay a tax to the state treasurer, as per the levy of the auditor. This meant a big savings to the state. Roads hauling Pullman or other sleeping cars were made liable for a tax on the same.

Public opinion concerning the Pullman company had about the same tone as it did in matters pertaining to the railroads. Governor Martin in his message of 1887 voiced this feeling very well when he said: "Foreign corporations should be forced to pay a tax on cars used in the carrying trade of Kansas. The Pullman Car Company has never paid a dollar of tax in Kansas. The tax-dodging practiced by these wealthy corporations is not only an outrage on the people who are compelled to bear burdens thus shirked, but is insulting to the dignity and authority of the state." But the climax of objurgation was not reached till the attorney general was heard from. "Notwithstanding the fact," he said, in speaking of the Pullman company, "that this great corporation has spread its arms out all over this country like a

[22] *First Ann. Report R. R. Commissioners*, p. 28, 29.

colossal octopus, and is sapping the life out of a traveling public by a system of exorbitant and fixed rates for accommodations, and with its army of half-paid employes, it declines to pay taxes in any State or Territory, except the state of its domicile.''[23]

The matter of paying taxes was forced upon this company for the first time in 1886, by the state board of railroad assessors. A stubborn fight was made in the courts to evade this tax altogether, but the attempt at evasion was unsuccessful. The Pullman company brought suit in the United States Circuit Court, District of Kansas, praying that county treasurers be enjoined from collecting any tax from this company. The bill of complaint claimed; (1) that the company's domicile and place of business was in Cook county, Illinois, and there was the situs of all its personal property;. (2) that the company was not subject to taxation in Kansas; and (3) that it was engaged in interstate commerce.[24]

The company further set forth that the board of railroad assessors, ''in violation of duty, wrongfully and unlawfully assumed to and did assess and value at $116,246.56 for purpose of taxation the property of said company used in Kansas.'' There was accordingly levied a ''large and burdensome tax, in the aggregate amounting to more than $3,000.''

The matter was pending before the courts for four years, and then the decision was handed down by the United States Supreme Court, to the effect that cars employed in interstate commerce may be taxed.[25] Kansas accordingly *pro rated* a tax on Pullman cars in proportion to the miles run in Kansas as compared with total mileage. The earning capacity of the cars was not taken into consideration, but simply their cost of construction as ordinary articles of personal property. A further analysis of this method will be given in a later chapter.

Municipal Finance.—Municipal financial matters during this period were involved largely in aid of railroads, as we have just seen. This was the principal object of expenditure. Other ob-

---

[23] *Report of Attorney General*, 1887-88.
[24] *Ibid.*
[25] 141 *U. S,.* 621.

jects for which debts were contracted, were city halls, waterworks, county courthouses, jails, bridges, and school houses. The
preponderance of railway aid over other forms of debt-increase
is however, characteristic of this period.

The early state laws contemplated a policy of paying all municipal indebtedness when due, and not the refunding of these
debts. But the magnitude of these debts became much greater
than had been anticipated. Accordingly, the legislature in 1879
passed a law enabling municipalities to refund their indebtedness. This applied to bonded indebtedness only. But these
local divisions interpreted it as meaning power to ''compromise
and refund their matured and maturing indebtedness of every
kind and description whatsoever, upon such terms as could be
agreed upon, and to issue new bonds * * * in payment for any
sums so compromised.''[26] Bonds were thus issued to pay for
county-seat wars, and to meet other extravagant and unauthor-
ized expenditures.

---

[26] *Message of Gov. Martin,* 1889.

CHAPTER VII

MUNICIPAL SUBSIDIES AND DEBTS, 1889–1902

The general features of this period may well be passed briefly in review, before entering upon a detailed discussion of the strictly financial subjects. This period is remarkable for the piling up of huge debts by the local divisions of the state. The state debt, under the constitutional limit of $1,000,000, can never be of any serious importance to the people, especially as population increases. But here at this time we find the municipal debts running up to a grand total of over $37,000,000. That is, the interest alone on this indebtedness was annually three times as large as the whole state debt. It is evident from this that "government of the people, by the people and for the people" comes more and more to mean government through the local divisions of the state. This entails a larger debt on the people even than the federal government, as is shown in Appendix E. The one significant thing about municipal debts and municipal subsidies, evidenced throughout this period, is the fact that inasmuch as they lacked any constitutional limitations, they lacked any fixed limitations whatever. For the changing limits set by the state legislatures fluctuated with each recurring session, and even such general regulations as were enacted were emasculated by numerous special exemptions. Evidence in support of this declaration is adduced in a paragraph below on the subject of municipal finance.

The decade, 1880 to 1890, was one of rapid growth for the commonwealth of Kansas, and this seemed to breed a spirit of speculation and adventure. Population increased 43 per cent., reaching 1,427,096 in 1890; the assessed valuation of the state in the same time increased 116.5 per cent. and the amount of capital invested in manufactures 302 per cent. But the reaction was sudden and sharp. Hard times set in about 1890, followed by three or four years of poor crops. The value of all agricultural products in 1894 was only $113,000,000, as against $147,000,000 ten years before.[1] Discontent spread among the farmers. The railroad bonds voted in the late sixties and early seventies were coming due. This led the farmers to lift their voices against the railroads and ask for rate reduction. In 1888 the Farmers' Alliance waxed strong, being a movement similar to the Grange which had died a few years before. In 1890 the Farmers' Alliance came out in politics as the People's Party or Populists. Two years later they elected a governor, and also a majority in the state senate. They stood for radical reforms in railway legislation and in general state economy, claiming that what was needed was a reduction in all taxes. One innovation they attempted in the way of reform was to enact the Ten Commandments into a state statute, with penalties attached.[2]

The financial panic of 1893 bore heavily upon Kansas. Many railroads were placed in the hands of receivers. Bank failures were numerous. Mortgage indebtedness on farm property was enormous. This represented large investments of eastern capital, and with the money panic came a pressure from the East for the payment of these mortgages in gold. The populists of Kansas were desperately in earnest over the free silver issue and were willing to stake their all on the success of the "cause." Many had come to translate their lack of capital as being simply a lack of silver, and hence they warmly took sides for the white metal. To protect themselves, the farmers secured the passage of the "Gold Mortgage Clause" law, providing that all mortgages and debts to be paid in money should be payable in either the standard silver or gold coins authorized by Congress, all stipulations in the contract to the contrary notwithstanding.[3] Whether this legislative fiat on the currency question really entered the domain of private contract and did any good admits of very

---

[1] 13 Bien. Report, State Board of Agr., Part VI, p. 1040.
[2] House Bill 898, Legislature 1897. Bill read second time and referred to Judiciary Committee; died there.
[3] Laws of 1893, ch. 99.

serious doubt. Industrial conditions soon changed for the better, so that the danger, supposed to be averted by this act, no longer existed. Mortgage indebtedness also gradually decreased. But the weight of this burden in the early part of this period was simply startling, and shows that there were some just causes for the wail of calamity that went up all over the state. In 1890 there was one mortgage in force for every family of five persons in the state.[4] The mortgage debt *per capita* was $170. If we add this private debt to the public debts resting upon each person in the state, we have a grand total of $210.35.[5] For the average family of five persons, this meant an indebtedness of over $1,000. The per cent. of incumbered land in the United States was 28.86, while in Kansas it was 60.32 per cent.

After the panic of 1893–94 came a season of good crops and good prices. Following the legislative session of 1897—a populistic administration—the People's Party rapidly disintegrated.

The tax laws and other financial matters of this period show some interesting developments which will now be discussed with some particularity.

Tax Laws.—Discontent with the various tax laws grew steadily during this time. The method of assessment by township trustees came in for a particular share of criticism. Many were in favor of a county assessor with deputies. Discussing the evils of existing methods, Governor Martin (1889) said, "But it is certain that a more unfair, inadequate and objectionable system than that now provided by our laws cannot be devised. Any change, therefore, would be an improvement." Others blamed the administration of the law, rather than the law itself. Governor Morrill condemned the system of township assessors elected for one year. "Now," says he "we have about sixteen hundred assessors, largely men with little practical experience, selected more because they have nothing else to do and are 'good fellows,' each trying to keep his assessment down so that his township may pay less than its honest share of the taxes."[6]

---

[4] *Eleventh Census.* Volume *Real Estate Mortgages.*
[5] Munic., debt., 25.57; State debt., 0.56; and U. S. debt., $14.22.
[6] *Message of Gov. Morrill,* 1895.

Public interest in tax reform had become crystallized enough
by the year 1901 to call for the creation of a state tax commission.[7] This was a temporary commission of eight able men,
appointed for the purpose of making a careful and full revision
of the tax laws of the state. They were to formulate a new tax
bill, embodying the results of their labor. The object of the
bill was to be, the statute declared, to secure uniformity in the
valuation and assessment of all taxable property in the state;
to secure the return and assessment of all taxable property at
its full and current valuation; and to simplify the methods of
assessment, levy, and collection of taxes. After some seven
months' investigation this commission reported a tax bill of
252 sections, based, for the most part, on the Indiana statute.
While this bill did not propose a complete revolution in the
existing system, yet it did intend to introduce some radical
changes directly in line with modern tendencies in taxation.
Each proposed change, however, was dictated by a crying need
of reform in the existing system. The chief new features of
this bill were, briefly, the following. A permanent state tax
commission was to be created, consisting of two men with a four
year term of service. Each county was to have a county assessor, appointed by the county board, and this county assessor
was to have a corps of deputy assessors, selected by the joint
action of himelf and the county board. In this manner a per-
fectly supervised system of assessment was to be provided with
a central, directing body at the state capitol. The general property tax was to be retained, since the constitution required this.
Telegraph, telephone, and express companies were to be assessed
no longer solely on the small amount of their tangible property
employed in the states, but on a basis of their earning capacity
as indicated by the amount of their stocks and bonds. Their
local real estate and personal property was still to be left for
local assessment, and to be subtracted from their full market
value as determined by the state board. The amount of this
total market value to be apportioned to Kansas depended on the
proportion of mileage in Kansas as compared with total mileage
operated. Ocean mileage of express companies was apparently

---

[7] *Laws of 1901*, ch. 361.

not to be excluded. The chief innovation of the bill was to be a state inheritance tax of 5 per cent. on collateral inheritances. Many other changes were proposed, but they were of secondary importance.

The bill went before the legislature of 1903, and was discussed throughout the session. The following points took up by far the greater part of the time: shall property be assessed at its full value; shall money, notes and mortgages, and other evidences of debt be exempt from taxation; shall the state funds remain in the county treasuries of the respective counties until actually needed by the state; shall a state tax commission be created; shall we have a county or township assessor.

The bill passed both houses with a few amendments, but the houses could not concur in the amendment providing for the state funds to remain in the county treasuries until actually needed. The trouble did not lie with the bill, but in the fact that one faction of the Republican party had control of the Senate and another of the House. So the bill did not become a law. "Hence," to quote a member of the commission that prepared the bill, "in this State more than one-half of the property goes untaxed."[8]

Real constructive work in tax legislation amounted to very little during this period. The most pronounced gain was the creation of a state board of assessors for the telegraph and telephone companies of the state.[9] The rapid extension of long-distance telephone service made this step imperatively necessary. The redemption of real estate sold for taxes, which, in 1876 reached the maximum penalty of 50 per cent., was now lowered once more, and fixed at 15 per cent.[10] This was thought expedient, since the delinquent tax list was steadily declining and the use of a heavy penalty was no longer needed.

Income.—The regular income of the state during this period came principally, as usual, from the direct general property tax. About 96 per cent. came from this source, and 4 per cent.

---

[8] Personal Letter of Hon. John Francis, of Kans. House of Representatives. Dec. 14, 1903.

[9] *Gen'l. Statutes*, 1899, ch. 107, sec. 5.

[10] *Gen'l. Statutes*, 1899, ch. 107, sec. 19.

'from small fees on insurance companies, oil inspection, bank in-spection, etc.

The tax rate was lowered, steadily, till the panic of 1893 caused a big slump in values, and then the old rate would not raise sufficient revenue. This decline in state values began in 1890 and continued in a more or less unbroken course for eleven years. This meant necessarily an increase in the tax rate. These fluctuations are clearly shown in the following table:

TOTAL ASSESSED VALUATIONS, LEVY AND RATE OF STATE TAXES, 1889-1902

Year.	Assessed valuations.	State levy.	Rate in mills.
1889	$360,815,073	$1,515,423	$4\frac{9}{10}$
1890	348,459,944	1,480,955	$4\frac{1}{4}$
1891	342,632,407	1,353,398	$3\frac{19}{25}$
1892	342,682,846	1,336,371	$3\frac{9}{10}$
1893	356,621,818	1,358,060	$3\frac{14}{10}$
1894	337,501,722	1,316,258	$3\frac{9}{10}$
1895	329,939,031	1,402,240	$4\frac{1}{4}$
1896	321,216,933	1,365,171	$4\frac{1}{4}$
1897	325,370,232	1,333,954	$4\frac{1}{10}$
1898	325,889,747	1,346,126	$4\frac{1}{10}$
1899	327,165,520	1,401,799	$5\frac{1}{2}$
1900	328,729,008	1,807,898	$5\frac{1}{2}$
1901	363,156,045	1,997,304	$5\frac{1}{2}$
1902	363,163,630	1,997,354	$5\frac{1}{2}$

There were a few small extraordinary expenses provided for at this time by the sale of bonds. These were for the industrial work of the state at the state penitentiary and will be spoken of at greater length under the subject of fiscal affairs below.

Expenditures.—Under the subject of expenditures, we have noted up to this point an interesting and rapid growth in the range of objects of state aid and state support. During this period we see a similar expansion. More attention is given to the immaterial wants, such as literature, science, art, etc.. than was formerly done. This we see indicated in the state expenditures for traveling libraries, an academy of science, a battle monument at Chickamauga, etc. For the first time we find the state granting a private pension, $600 a year, after the manner of the federal government. For the material development of the state, a board of irrigation is made an object of public expenditure in 1895. An important new commission for the supervision of banks is created in 1891. This matter of state supervision is further extended by the appointment of a grain inspector and an oil inspector.

These new activities of the state denote certain important phases of growth. Both the material and immaterial wants are expanding. The growth follows no fixed principle, each new question that arises touching the proper function of the state being dealt with empirically by the legislature then in session. The tendency is plainly manifest, however, for the strong, eastern part of the state to be taxed for the benefit of the weak western portion. Evidence of this is observable in the relief to frontier settlers, forestry bureaus, board of irrigation, sugar subsidies, etc. In the 1902 budget we even find an appropriation of $5,000 for the extermination of prairie dogs and gophers, which amount to pests in the western part of the state. The theory of the legislators seems to be that the state is a unit, and when one member suffers, the others suffer with it. And thus. insurance is wisely provided against avoidable hardships.

The year 1890 was marked by drought and a general crop failure throughout the western part of the state. The legislature appropriated $60,000 to purchase seed grain for distribution among the needy settlers. This was not, however, a donation by any means. County commissioners were to draw warrants against their counties for the grain received, these warrants to be due and payable one year later, and to be turned over to the state treasurer. The county commissioners were to sell the grain to the farmers on their note, running one year at 6 per cent. interest. Of this fund, $56,428 was used as intended. Coal was also contributed from the state mine, worth $4,211. It is due to the railroads to say that the principal roads generously hauled this coal free of charge.

The year 1894 was another period of severity for the frontier settlers. And again the state came to their relief. Two thousand dollars was appropriated for the purchase of coal for distribution among the needy of that section, and $100,000 for the purchase of seed grain.

In 1897 the act promoting silk culture was repealed, and the policy of fostering this industry by the state was abandoned. The irrigation and forestry bureaus were combined, since they sought ends so much similar.

The state outlay in subsidies to private charities began with one institution in 1870. By 1880, the number had increased to 4; and by 1902, 21 institutions were on the list, each claiming to be as necessary as the others, and therefore entitled to state aid.[11] None is subject to state supervision. The average yearly subsidy for each institution is $900.

An interesting chapter in the state's budget is that pertaining to the state's experience in protecting the infant industry of beet sugar manufacture. The policy of a state subsidy was launched in 1887,[12] but the legislature forgot to make an appropriation till the next session, two years later. A bounty of two cents a pound was provided for all beet and sorghum sugar made in the state from plants grown in the state. The industry made quite a spurt, and promised big things for the future. The bounty claimed and paid in 1891 was over $50,000. In that year a populistic legislature stood out for retrenchment in all lines of expenditure, and accordingly, the rate of bounty was cut down to $\frac{3}{4}$ of a cent a pound. Evil days then befell the

---

[11] Names of these private charities in chronological order:
  Home for Friendless Women, Leavenworth,
  Orphans' Asylum, Leavenworth,
  St. Vincent's Orphan Asylum, Leavenworth,
  Kansas Orphans' Home, Leavenworth,
  Samaritan Mission,
  Christ's Hospital, Topeka,
  Atchison City Hospital,
  Topeka Orphans' Home,
  St. Francis' Hospital, Wichita,
  St. Margaret's Hospital, Kansas City,
  Mercy Hospital, Fort Scott,
  Bethany Hospital, Kansas City,.
  City Hospital, Wichita,
  Old Ladies' Rest, Leavenworth,
  Home of the Friendless, Parsons,
  Wichita Children's Home,
  Kansas Protective Home. Association, Leavenworth,
  Rescue Home, Kansas City,
  Pittsburg Hospital,
  Kansas Children's Home Society, Topeka,
  Mother Bickerdyke Home and Hospital, Ellsworth.
[12] *Laws of 1887*, ch. 231.

infant industry. In a few years the bounty was entirely removed. Then came a further decline in the industry, and in 1897 the last piece of sugar machinery was sold and sent to Nebraska where the business was still on its feet.

The actual amount of bounty paid for beet sugar by the state is shown in this brief table:

SUGAR BOUNTIES PAID

1889	$18,658 30
1891	50,304 08
1892	3,000 00
1893	15,303 83
1895	7,339 29
1896	5,331 00
Total	$99,936 50

But the irrigation region in western Kansas gave promise of great possibilities along the sugar-beet culture line. And sugar factories were in operation across the Colorado line. So the legislature of 1901 provided for a bounty of $1 a ton on all sugar beets grown in the state, abandoning the idea of stimulating any more home sugar factories. The limit of this beet bounty was set by law at $5,000 in any one year. The bounties paid in 1901 amounted to $1,747.36. The beet farmers this year reported a net profit of $17.08 per acre.[13]

Fiscal Affairs.—In the management of fiscal affairs during this period the state worked out a new problem for herself in connection with the public industries at the state prison. It was decided to employ the prisoners at useful labor on the state's account, and in industries competing least with free labor, especially union labor. To this end a binder twine plant was established, the market in view being primarily the wheatgrowers of the state. The coal mine, employing from 250 to 400 men, was designed to furnish coal to state institutions only. A brick plant is now operated for the same purpose. But binder twine was intended for the open market, which, as was correctly ex-

---

[13] *13 Bien. Report Bureau of Agriculture,* p. 1118.

pected, was found with the farmers. An enormous plant with elaborate machinery was installed. The purchase of manila fiber and other raw materials represented a heavy initial investment, but only for a short time, for there was a ready market for the finished product. To purchase raw materials, therefore, a "revolving fund" was created, as it was called. Bond issues in amounts from $5,000 to $50,000 were made, the bonds bearing 4 per cent. interest and running one year or less. These were purchased by the uninvested moneys in the permanent school fund. In 1900, $60,000 of one-year bonds were issued to provide for this revolving fund. There was also an issue of $50,000 which was paid that same year.

It was during this period that a deficit again occurred in the treasury. The funds therein were all in the nature of "balances" of specific funds, and hence not available for use on the general revenue fund. This is in accordance with the constitutional requirement that no money shall be paid out except on specific appropriations. This leaves the alternatives of borrowing or letting state warrants run on interest when stamped unpaid. Both methods were used. The interest paid on stamped warrants in 1901 was only $12, but in 1902 it was $8,690.66. This deficit was usually due to the reluctancy of each administration to raise the levy for state taxes over that of preceding administrations, for an increase in the levy was likely to provoke charges of prodigality. This has become a custom, although the expanding needs of the state institutions constantly call for increased expenditures.

This period presented the anomaly of having both large deficits and large balances. But, as before explained, the balances could not be applied to the deficiencies. The question of the disposition of these idle sums came in for much discussion by those interested in state finances at this time. Many able thinkers, including Governor Stanley, held that these funds should be deposited largely in private banks throughout the state, at interest, thus securing an income for the state and providing an increased circulation of money. The average balance on hand in the capital city was over one-half million dollars annually. This at 3 per cent. interest would represent an annual income to the state of $15,000, besides increasing the circulating medium for the state at large. The extent of these balances is shown in the table below.[14]

TREASURY BALANCES, 1888–1902.

Year.	Balance.	Year.	Balance.
1888	$324.882	1896	$604,529
1889	338,746	1897	363,026
1890	715,138	1898	412,152
1891	461,502	1899	498,450
1892	727,163	1900	510,711
1893	895,540	1901	577.626
1894	842,326	1902	627,367
1895	710,415		

The permanent school fund, in spite of its safeguards, was several times encumbered with small issues of bogus bonds from frontier school districts. The size of this fund made it a difficult one to administer well and keep invested profitably. School district bonds now became the prevailing securities bought, since the supply of state bonds was running short. In December, 1900, this fund reached a total of $7,060,821.73, and was all invested but $68,344.46.[15]

The permanent funds were invested in bonds held by the state treasurer as follows:

Permanent school fund $6,643,297 44
University permanent fund ....,..... 148,260 82
Normal school permanent fund............... 200,919 01

Total $6,992,477 27

The uninvested funds at the same time were:

Permanent school fund $63,650 24
University permanent fund 969 17
Normal school permanent fund 3,725 05

Total $68,344 46

The source of these funds, as noted before, was almost entirely the school lands which were sold from time to time. The sell-

[14] 13 Bien. Report, State Treasurer.
[15] 12 Bien. Report, Supt. of Public Instruction.

ing price in the early periods was extremely low, since there were so few settlers in the state. The amount of these lands sold and the price are presented in the following table:

SCHOOL LANDS PATENTED, 1861–1902.[16]

Common School Lands, 1861–1902:
         1,522,322 acres: $5,534,642 97: average $3 63
Agricultural College Lands, 1868–1895:
         78.046 76 acres: $458,881 91: average $5 88
University Lands, 1878–1902.
         43,713 79 acres: $130,469 16: average $2 98
Normal School Lands, 1876–1902:
         40,737 38 acres: $213,514 71: average $5 24

The University has the lowest endowment and has made the poorest showing in the average price per acre for lands sold. This small endowment means a greater dependence on the bounty and generosity of the state legislature.

Municipal Finances.—The fever of voting municipal aid ran extremely and dangerously high at this time. All former records were surpassed; constraints were brushed aside. The executive messages for years fulminated against the growing burdens of municipal indebtedness, but all to no purpose. The announcement of crushing tax levies failed to terrorize the voters. Buoyant faith in the unbroken prosperity and development of their community led them to hypothecate a large share of their future income. This spirit became rampant during the years from 1886 to 1888, when the local debts were piled up to a sum forty times as large as the state debt.

The bulk of this debt was incurred as subsidies to railroads, but in the early '90's came an overwhelming reaction. Local aid was then directed to industries of a more purely private nature, and the Supreme Court decision of 1873 was apparently forgotten.

An idea of the nature and magnitude of municipal aid during the years 1886, 1887 and 1888 can best be gained by examining a few typical cases. Seven counties are accordingly given in the tabular statement below, together with some of their minor subdivisions. This shows the preponderance, at

[16] *13 Bien. Report, Auditor of State,* 1902.

this time, of railroad aid, the significance of the debt-burden when compared with population and total taxable property, and also serves to accentuate the transition from railroad subsidies to private subsidies.

MUNICIPAL DEBT INCREASE, 1886–1888.

County.	Population 11th census.	Taxable property.	Total increase in debt.	Increase for railroads.	Railroad Aid Debt in specified municipalities.
Cowley.........	34,478	$6,906,587	$382,500	$285,000	County.......... $100,000 3 cities .... 88,500 6 townships 97,000
Chautauqua ..	12,297	2,090,860	275,000	275,000	County.......... 140,000 7 townships 135,000
Dickinson	22,273	5,130,192	361,500	332.500	County..... ..... 233,000 5 townships. ... 64,000 1 city.... 35,000
Kingman......	11,823	3,282,698	246,500	216,000	County........... 125,000 5 townships 91,500
Kiowa.........	2,873	1,647,581	188,000	170,000	County.......... 170,000
Ness..........	4,944	1,870,200	164,500	164,500	County.......... 75,000 6 townships ..... 77,000 1 city 12,500
Republic......	19,002	3,154,382	92,500	92,500	....

This marked the close of the era of large subsidies to railroads. Discussion of this, however, must be postponed to the paragraph on railroads below. But this marked the beginning only of a period of excessive municipal grants to general industries of a public, semi-public, and private nature. The court decision of 1873, as was previously mentioned, put a temporary check on public aid to private industries. Subsequent decisions were in harmony with this opinion. For instance, the Kansas Supreme Court held (in *Gilmore v. Norton*, 10 *Kans.*, 491) that an "act conferring such [corporate] powers limited in its operations to a single city is manifestly a special act conferring corporate powers and is void, being forbidden by section 1, article 12, of the constitution."

The general laws obtaining throughout this period conferred rather liberal powers, even had they been strictly observed. But they were not closely followed, as numerous special acts show. The General Statutes of 1889 authorized counties to issue

bonds for county buildings, deficits, relief, railroad aid, and sub-
scriptions to promote prospecting for coal, natural gas, artesian
wells, and to assist sugar and sorghum mills.[17]   Cities of the
first class (those having over 15,000 inhabitants) were limited
in their powers of taxation to the following levies:

(1) A tax for general revenue purposes, not to exceed 6 mills.

(2) A tax for general improvements, 6 mills.

(3) A tax for paying interest on indebtedness, to the necessary amount.

(4) A license tax upon all professions and occupations carried
on in the city.

Paving, sewerage, etc., require special assessments on abutting
property, and hence were not put under the above limitations.

Cities of the second class (those having between 2,000 and
15,000) were limited to a bonded debt of 10 per cent. of their
assessed valuation.   There was also a general provision made
that counties could pay bounties on wolf, coyote, wild cat, fox,
rabbit, crow, and gopher scalps.[18]   To promote forestry culture,
counties were authorized to give a bounty of $10 an acre for
each acre of timber set out and successfully cultivated for five
years.[19]

These, then, are the general laws on the statute books during
this period pertaining to municipal finances.   But these were
not sufficient to cover the wants of the people.   The desire for
special acts was irrepressible.   In the year 1889, for example,
Haskell county was authorized by a special law to make a bond
issue of $10,000.[20]   This is a frontier county, and hence it was
thought that development might be forced if only the initial
expense of breaking the sod was obviated.   So this bond issue
was authorized to provide a fund for paying a bounty of $1 an
acre for breaking sod in this county prior to October 1, 1889.

An examination of the statutes from this time on reveals an
almost indiscriminate voting of aid for purposes of drilling
gas wells, prospecting for oil and coal, erection of flour mills,
cheese factories, etc.   By some peculiarity of construction, the

---

[17] *General Statutes, 1889*, ch. 12a.
[18] *Laws of 1889*, chs. 89. 90, *Laws of 1895*, ch. 358.
[19] *Laws of 1889*, ch. 254.
[20] *Ibid.*, ch. 154.

voters seemed to consider a flour mill a public industry, although owned, operated and controlled by private individuals.

To consider briefly a few concrete cases, we may take the session laws of 1891.[21]

Cimarron township, Gray county, is authorized to issue bonds to build a flour mill. This same legislature authorized ten flour mills and three other private enterprises. The history of the Cimarron experiment is brief but striking, and is well exhibited in the session laws of 1897, six years after the flour mill experiment. Kansas at this time held $15,000 of Cimarron's bonds in her permanent school fund, due in August, 1902. In the statute pertaining to this case, we read the expressive words:[22] "Whereas, said city of Cimarron has a bonded indebtedness of $55,000 and a floating indebtedness of about $10,000, and is in default of interest due on bonds more than $15,000, making a total indebtedness of $80,000, and the property of all kinds in said city has an aggregate assessed valuation of only $31,351, and said city is insolvent and unable to pay but a small per cent. of its indebtedness * * * therefore * * * the mayor and council of said city desire to scale indebtedness of said city down to a sum upon which they can pay interest and ultimately pay the principal." A compromise was accordingly authorized and effected.

To go back to the year 1889 again—the record of municipal aid this year is interesting. One township is authorized to aid a milling company erect a flour mill by voting $15,000 of 6 per cent. bonds, running 20 and 30 years. For prospecting for coal and gas, three townships are permitted to vote $5,000 each; one $1,500; another, $8,000 of 7 per cent. bonds. One city is allowed to vote $15,000 to aid a college situated within its limits.

The legislature of 1893 authorized two townships to vote $5,000 each in 6 per cent. bonds in aid of flour mills. The next legislature gave permission for one township to extend $3,000 of aid to flour-mill enterprise. The auditor's bond register for 1900 shows a similar record for municipalities all over the state. Gray county, for example, shows a bond registry

---

[21] *Laws of 1891*, ch. 44.
[22] *Laws of 1897*, ch. 178.

of $15,000 for a sugar mill; $8,000 for a flour mill; and $2,000 for a cheese factory. Hamilton county shows $4,000 for a flour mill. Leavenworth county's record is $10,000 for a coal company and $15,000 for a gas well. The little city of Tonganoxie in this county even has $2,500 on her account for prospecting for coal. West Plains township in Meade county shows a bond registry of $15,000 for a sugar mill, the bonds running for 20 years at 6 per cent.

In nearly every case these mills and factories receiving artificial stimulus from the public funds proved a complete and dismal failure. It was simply a prostitution of the public money to uses which private capital in the hands of prudent, business-like investors avoided. But like a lottery, it proved seductive to the public, because there was one chance of winning, even if there were a hundred of losing. The little city of Anthony, Harper county, is a conspicuous example of a loser in this game of chance. She tried to force prosperity to bloom for her at once by mortgaging many years of her future. Like an individual who tries every get-rich-quick scheme that comes along, this little city lavishly voted aid to each promising enterprise that seemed likely to ensure her prosperity. But as was generally the case, this artificial stimulus failed to produce a healthful growth. Population decreased; assessed valuations fell off. The climax came in 1897, when, like Cimarron, the city was bankrupt and a humiliating compromise was granted by the state legislature.[23] Her tax levy for 1896 had reached the absurd limit of 13.4 per cent. of the total valuation. Of course this was more than could be paid. When the compromise was effected, and the debt-scaling commenced, the debt was $168,187.75, while the total assessed value of all property in the city was only $171,051. To collect this debt would, therefore, have required a clean sweep of the whole city.

The different steps in the insolvency of the city are easily seen in the table below:

---

[23] *Laws of 1897*, ch. 178.

DECLINE OF ANTHONY, KANSAS.[24]

Year.	Population.	Assessed valuation.
1889	2,252	$512,684 28
1890	2,021	473,167 82
1891	1,825	409,362 17
1892	2,003	355,490 67
1893	2,404	422,202 94
1894	1,686	252,421 31
1895	1,367	239,907 60
1896	1,074	171,051 00
1897	City insolvent,	debt $168,187 55.

This was not Anthony's first experience of this kind, neither was she alone in her financial straits, by any means. In December, 1896, the commissioners of Lane county formally declared the county insolvent, and issued instructions to the county treasurer to refrain from further payment of interest on the bonded indebtedness. The funded debt was $125,000, the population (11th census) only 2,055. This meant a burden of $304 per family.

It is instructive to take a general survey of the municipal debt of this period, with its change from year to year. The amount of debt incurred annually and the total debt for each year were appallingly large, as will be seen by an examination of the statement below:

MUNICIPAL DEBT, 1885-1902.[25]

Year.	Railroad bonds registered.	Refunding bonds registered.	Total bonds registered.	Total outstanding net debt.
1885-86	$961,000	$1,593,629	$3,172,390	$17,473,347
1887-88	8,544,551	2,378,750	13,338,062	30,733,935
1889-90	804,250	3,419,030	7,576,689	36,491,660
1891-92	315,000	1,154,240	3,271,831	37,075,740
1893-94	56,500	299,661	1,501,028	36,805,599
1895-96		712,900	1,719,677	34,604,246
1897-98	200,000	1,074,000	2,104,552	32,276,339
1899-1900	31,500	4,509,140	6,401,333	32,398,799
1901-02	59,000	2,398,602	2,724,100	32,614,909

Under refunding bonds, come all those originally issued for bridges, waterworks, schools, etc., but principally railroad bonds,

---

[24] *Commercial and Financial Chronicle*, (N. Y.) Feb. 20, 1897.
[25] Compiled from reports of Auditor and Board of R. R. Commissioners.

for these were far in the majority. The refunding column above shows an interesting tendency to postpone the payment of the debts well into the future instead of meeting them when due. Thus the last bond registry, that for 1901-02 shows that practically all the bonds issued during that biennium were refunding bonds. So in nearly every case above, the interest outlay is twice or three times the principal of the debt. While, therefore, the table shows a debt for 1902 of about $32,000,000, the real outlay represented is at least $64.000,000,or some $40 per capita. The municipalities continue to make very free use of the refunding privilege.

Banking.—It has been necessary to say but little thus far on the subject of banking. This is because the state made no attempt to regulate the business of banking prior to the passage of the banking law of 1891.[26] This law was repealed six years later, and a more elaborate and comprehensive one enacted in its place. There are thus three periods in Kansas banking history, namely, the period of unregulated banking, 1861 to 1891; the period of loose state supervision under a bank commission, 1891 to 1897; and finally, the present system of strict state supervision under an improved bank commission dating from 1897. The title of the 1891 law was, ''An act providing for the organization and regulation of banks, and prescribing penalties for violation of the provisions of this act.'' The more complete law of 1897 bears this title, ''An act relating to banks and banking; providing for the organization, management, control, regulation and supervision of banks; and providing penalties for violations of the provisions of this act, and repealing chapter 43 of the laws of 1891.''[27]

The principal feature of the 1891 law, and the one which survived in the 1897 law, was that providing for the appointment of a state bank commissioner. The law clothed this commissioner with certain powers and duties, among which were those of supervising all private and state banks in the commonwealth; of requiring at least four reports a year from each bank; and of taking charge of insolvent banks till receivers should be ap-

---

[26] *Laws of 1891*, ch. 43; 2 *Bien. Report Bank Commissioner*, 1893-94.
[27] *Genl. Stat.*, 1897, p. 187.

pointed. This commissioner or his deputy was to visit each bank in the state (except National banks) at least once a year and make a careful investigation. For this investigation the bank was to pay a fee fixed by law.[28] Other general provisions were that any five or more persons could organize a banking association; the capital stock should be at least $5,000, and half paid up before beginning business; the amount of money on hand in available funds was to be 20 per cent. of deposits, one-half of which might consist of balances due from good, solvent banks, and one-half of cash on hand.

This law made no provision concerning the amount of real estate a bank could own and list as part of its paid up capital. The new law corrected this oversight. In it the provision is made that banks may hold and dispose of real estate acquired in the collection of debts, but no bank may hold real estate in excess of 50 per cent. of its capital. This ensures an element of fluidity in the bank's assets which the earlier law entirely overlooked. The banker in the small Kansas town is expected to be an investor in each new enterprise undertaken in his community, be it a street railway, gas or electric company, creamery, cheese factory, woolen mill, opera house, or what not. These investments usually prove business failures to the initial investors. To safeguard against such a use of bank funds, the 1897 law provides that no bank shall employ its moneys, directly or indirectly, in trade or commerce. This law also makes some changes in the legal reserves requirement. Banks in cities of less than 5,000 inhabitants must have available funds on hand to the amount of 20 per cent. of their total deposits, and in cities of over 5,000 population an amount equal to 25 per cent. of their entire deposits. But in the latter case, one-half the reserve may consist in balances due from other banks, and one-half in actual money. Full publicity of the bank's affairs is sought through a personal examination, and through the statement, made at irregular intervals, upon call, four times a year. This statement, submitted to the bank commissioner and also published in the local

---

[28] Fee for examination:
$10 for bank with capital stock of $5,000.
$15 for bank with capital stock of $5,000 to $50,000.
$20 for bank with capital stock of over $50,000.

newspaper sets forth in detail under appropriate heads the resources and liabilities of the bank. This is similar to the report
required of national banks by the comptroller. Two deputies
are allowed the commissioner, under the 1897 law, and to meet
the increased expense of the department, the fees for examination are increased.[29]

Savings banks are also mentioned in this law, although they
are new and comparatively unimportant in Kansas. Provision
is made that any five or more persons may organize one, and the
capital stock must not be less than $50,000 nor more than
$500,000, 10 per cent. of which must be paid up when sub-
scribed.

The early bank commissioners took the position that a general
"house-cleaning" among the banks was needed, and they went
at their work accordingly. The evils of overdrafts, excessive
loans, heavy real estate investments, inadequate reserves, etc.,
were lopped off as far as was practicable. "The pruning
process," says one commissioner, "the scaling down of assets,
has been severe and occasionally a vigorous protest has been
made."[30] During the panic of 1893, when the banks of New York
resorted to payment in clearing house certificates, the commissioner took the position that such banks were not such as this
law contemplated as depositories for the reserve of Kansas
banks. Hence he issued an order to the effect that until the New
York banks should again resume payment in lawful money,
deposits therein in excess of 2 per cent. of the total deposits of the
bank making the same would not be considered a part of their
legal reserve. The order created considerable alarm and evoked
much newspaper comment. Many people supposed Kansas banks
were indebted to New York banks to a large amount. But this
indebtedness proved to be only about $150,000, while at the
same time the Kansas banks had over $500,000 on deposit in
New York.[31]

---

[29] Fees under 1897 law:
    Bank's capital $15,000 or less, fee $15.
    Bank's capital $15,000 to $25,000, fee $20.
    Bank's capital $25,000 to $50,000, fee $25.
    Bank's capital $50,000 to $100,000, fee $30.
    Bank's capital $100,000+, fee $35.
[30] 4 Bien. Report, Bank Commissioner, 1898.
[31] 2 Bien. Report, Bank Commissioner, 1893-94.

The item of overdrafts was cut down 62½ per cent. in eighteen months after January, 1893. Bills payable and rediscounts were reduced 65 per cent. in the same time.

Some abuses crept in under the section of the 1897 law providing for the reorganization of banks as state banks. Several national banks, on the verge of ruin, reorganized under this provision, and failed soon afterwards. Their capital was greatly reduced under their reorganization, this reducing, *pari passu*, their stockholders' liability, while the banks' liability to their creditors remained unchanged. Thus when the fall came, the stockholders were ready to escape with a minimum of loss to themselves and a maximum of loss to their creditors.

Commissioners discourage private banks, on the ground that death of the owner forces a closing of the bank, and that the owner is likely to engage in various unsafe enterprises. As a result, these decrease in number, while state and national banks increase. The following table illustrates this change:

NUMBER OF BANKS IN KANSAS, 1896-1902.

	1896	1898	1900	1902
State banks	283	286	334	426
Private banks	109	82	55	38
National banks	116	101	111	146

The condition of the Kansas banks from 1891 to 1902 may be summarized from the commissioners' reports. A decrease in the number of banks, it will be seen, did not always mean a falling off in the total resources.

SUMMARY OF THE CONDITION OF KANSAS STATE AND PRIVATE BANKS, 1891-1902.

Date.	Number of banks.	Total resources.
1891, Oct. 13	414	$30,257,981
1892, Sept. 1	447	34,637,146
1893, Oct. 3	420	28,806,786
1894, July 18	410	28,738,013
1895, July 11	408	27,934,977
1896, Sept. 1	392	25,691,882
1897, Oct. 5	383	31,555,466
1898, July 14	364	31,010,378
1899, Sept. 7	383	35,093,991
1900, Sept. 1	388	40,911,240
1901, Sept. 30	422	53,288,205
1902, Sept. 2	462	51,216,829

The panic of '93 and '94, together with the purging process of
the commissioners, made the heavy reduction in the number of
banks noticeable above. How much was due to each cause would
be difficult to determine.

A peculiar feature now in vogue in the commissioners' reports
is the "roll of honor," that is, a list of state and private banks
that have an unimpaired surplus equal to or greater than 50
per cent. of their capital. The list is rapidly growing, whether
it be the cause or effect of the "roll of honor." The 1902 roll
comprised 21 per cent. of all state and private banks in the commonwealth.

The movement towards sound banking has been very pronounced since the passage of the 1897 law. Banks in general hold
little else but clean assets, convertible into cash readily at the
value at which they are carried on the books. The heaviest
losses charged off in this movement have been bad paper (about
a million and a half dollars since 1897), and depreciation in
real estate (about half a million dollars).

All this has been accomplished without any expense to the
state, since the fees of the banking department are more than
sufficient for its maintenance.

Building and loan associations were not put under the supervision of the bank commissioner till 1899.[32] At that time the
need of such a step was well established. Many associations ob-
jected strenuously to the full publicity given their tranactions
by the new law, but the public was as much pleased as it was
benefited. Under the provisions of this act, whenever the bank
commissioner deemed a concern "unsafe and inexpedient" for
carrying on further business, he promptly wound up its affairs.
Under this heroic treatment, the number of "national" or
foreign associations in the state rapidly diminished, while the
number of sound locals increased. A full set of fees was applied to foreign associations, ranging from $100 for application

---

[32] *Laws of 1899*, ch. 78.

for admission to the state, to $1 for affixing the commissioner's seal and certifying any paper.[33]

The atmosphere of publicity given these associations has proved thoroughly salutary for the public concerned, and is doubtless indicative of the tendency towards greater publicity in other lines of industry.

Railroads.—This period in the state's history was one of unusually hard times for the railroads, due principally to the extravagant overstimulus given them in the preceding period. The roads had overbuilt. Mileage exceeded all normal business demands. A reaction set in early in the '90's. In 1896 but two roads out of twenty-six paid any dividends, while thirteen were in the hands of receivers. Many miles of road went out of use altogether, so that the total mileage was less in 1900 than in 1890, although the material resources of the state had made a considerable gain. The roads were a burden to their owners and to the taxpayers of the commonwealth who had voted them bonds. The total cash and land subsidies granted these roads up to 1902 amounted to $43,700,000, whereas the taxes they had paid into the state and municipal treasuries amounted to only $42,000,000.[34] Disappointment was pronounced throughout the state, especially in those communities that had paid dearly for the roads and had not realized the anticipated benefits. The decrease in mileage and the diminution in local aid are tabulated in the statement below:

---

[33] Fees for foreign building and loan associations:
  Application for admission to state.........................$100
  Certificate of authority (or renewal which may be annual at option of bank commissioner)............................ $50
  Filing semi-annual statement (assets under $50,000), $3; (assets $50,000 to $100,000) $5; (assets $100,000 to $250,000) $10; ($250,000 to $500,000) $20; ($500,000 to $1,000,000) $30; ($1,000,000+) $50.

[34] Cash Subsidies=$10,837,686.
  Land (at $3½ per acre)=$32,880,670.
  Taxes from auditor's reports, and estimated for early years=$41,791,746.

RAILROAD MILEAGE, YEARLY INCREASE OR DECREASE, AND SUBSIDY.

Year.	Mileage main track.	Increase.	Decrease.	Subsidy, biennial periods.
1888	8,312	2100	....	....
1889	8,721	409	....	$804,250
1890	8,763	43	....	
1891	8,853	90	....	315,000
1892	8,845	....	8	
1893	8,840	....	5	56,500
1894	8,832	....	8	
1895	8,829	....	3	0
1896	8,829	0	0	
1897	8,80?	....	27	200,000
1898	8,759	....	43	
1899	8,690	....	69	31,500
1900	8,717	27	....	
1901	8,710	....	7	59,000
1902	8,754	44	....	

The farmers of the state laid a large share of the blame for hard times on the railroads. They accused these carriers of unjust discrimination in rates against the Kansas shippers. "More state control" became the political cry of the populist party. They legislated accordingly, but found that the courts would not suffer an interference with interstate commerce. Governor Lewelling, speaking of the powers of the state railroad commission, and chafing under federal restraints on state action said, "Here then is the Scylla and Charybdis of legislative action: the inefficacy of too little power on the one hand, and the unconstitutionality of too much power on the other hand."[35] A way around this difficulty was sought in the closing days of the populist régime, when Governor Leedy called a special session of the legislature in December, 1898, a few days only before the time for the regular sessions. The law of 1883 creating the board of railroad commissioners was repealed, and in its place the legislature hastily created a "Court of Visitation" with certain judicial and administrative powers. But this court, so-called, was short-lived, for the law was almost immediately put to the test of the courts and there held unconstitutional. This left the state for a period of two years (April, 1899, to March, 1901.) without any board. A new board similar to the first, was created by the legislature of 1901.

[35] *Message of Gov. Lewelling*, 1893.

A movement in favor of a state railroad gained considerable headway at this time, culminating, however, only in talk. Governor Leedy in 1897, impatient at the decisions of the Supreme Court and the impotency of the interstate commerce commission, suggested in his message that Kansas, Nebraska, and Texas should build their own road to the Gulf. The idea was popular with many people, but the majority thought it too visionary or socialistic. The constitution prohibits the state from ever being a *party* in carrying on any works of internal improvement, but whether the state can do such a work, not as a party, but as a principal, is a 'different question.

What little municipal aid was granted to railroads at this time was chiefly under special laws. For example, in 1893, we find Haskell county authorized to vote aid to the amount of $2,000 a mile within the county; while six townships in the same county are permitted to vote $2,000 a mile; that is, $4,000 a mile counting both grants.[36] The general limit set by the 1887 law, however, is $2,000 a mile.[37] In 1895 a city is allowed to vote bonds to the extent of $35,000, and has a special exemption from limitations of other acts.[38] Again this same year a township is authorized to vote $4,000 a mile to a railroad.[39]

And thus the general laws on the subject were made nugatory by special laws, as often as local interests dictated such a policy. While the constitution is silent on the limits of municipal indebtedness, it does expressly state that no special laws shall be passed. But this is a check which is inoperative.

The present system of assessment and taxation of railroads, Pullman cars, express companies, telegraph and telephone companies, will be considered in due order in the next chapter.

---

[36] *Laws of 1893*, chs. 44, 45.
[37] *Laws of 1887*, ch. 183.
[38] *Laws of 1895*, ch. 65.
[39] *Laws of 1895*, ch. 70.

CHAPTER VIII.

PRESENT FINANCIAL "SYSTEM"

There has been traced in the preceding pages the evolution of the present "system," or rather confusion, of tax regulations of the state. Attention has been directed to the gradual growth and extension of public expenditures, and also to the important features of state income. The financial history of the commonwealth has been wrought out under the popular pressure for "rigid economy." This has hampered the state in some of its spheres of work, such as public charities and higher education, but it has not prevented those smaller leaks that constantly sap the public revenues. Although the state has, in some lines, been forced into practices of parsimony, yet the municipalities have been free to spend their public funds with a lavish hand. Constitutional requirements have been a second force in shaping the state's financial affairs. These requirements have set limits to the extraordinary expenditures of the state, and have made necessary a certain so-called "uniformity" in matters of raising revenue. It now remains to examine with some particularity the significant features of the state's financial life of today; that is, the matters of expenditure, income, and general fiscal administration.

Outlay.—The outlay of the state determines its income, for the income is never adjusted till the amount of expenditure is determined upon. Hence primary importance attaches to the outlay which the state makes from year to year. The nature of these expenditures shows exactly what functions the state is exercising, and a study of these functions is a very fruitful one. But it will not be necessary at this point to go into such an investigation, after what has been given. A few general com-

ments must suffice.   It has already been recorded how, at the
very outset, the state performed only those essential duties
making for internal and external security.   This was done
through the machinery of the state government (administrative
officers such as governor, treasurer, auditor, secretary of state,
attorney, adjutant, superintendent of public instruction, and
others), the state legislature, and the state judiciary.   This included expenditures both for educational and penal institutions.
Works of benevolence and charity were taken up immediately
afterwards.   From this beginning there is noticeable a general expansion of state activities, calculated to promote the economic,
physical and intellectual interests of the people.   This growth
is manifest in the creation of state agricultural and horticultural
societies; fish commissions; silk commissions; live stock sanitary
commisssions; insurance department; bank commissioner; grain
and oil inspectors, etc., and in the granting of relief to frontier
settlers, the creation of a board of health, labor bureau, etc., and
finally in the support of an historical society; academy of sciences;
traveling libraries, etc.   Special needs have called forth the creation of temporary commissions, such as the beef combine commission of 1889, the tax commission of 1901, etc.

The present outlay of the state follows many channels.   The
table given below clearly shows the actual expenditures for 1901
and 1902, and the objects of the outlay.

STATE OUTLAY, 1901 AND 1902

Object.	1901.	1902.
State government (administrative)	$115,713	$122,282
Judiciary	158,003	159,896
Legislature	89,588	(No session.)
Higher education	308,608	393,308
Penitentiary	234,947	300,195
Public charities	889,585	825,716
Private charities	13,000	15,700
Literary and scientific objects	8,410	20,151
Pensions	600	600
State printing	127,500	71,900
Capitol and state property	112,969	131,681
Boards, supervising general health and industry of state	65,899	80,248
Destruction of prairie dogs		1,974
Quantrell raid claims		78,729
Sugar beet bounty		15,153
Miscellaneous	101,425	9,899
Totals	$2,227,855	2,258,594

But along with this outlay of the state there should be considered the expenditures of the local divisions, in order to see clearly how the public funds are employed. This will show, not only the cost of government, but also the specific objects for which this money is expended.

By returns made to the state auditor from the municipalities, it is easy to determine the rates of state and local taxes for any given year. By taking a large number of years and averaging returns, a fairly accurate statement is obtained of the different kinds of taxes paid by the people. Such an average made from a series of years gives the following interesting statement of per cents:

TOTAL STATE AND LOCAL TAXES

State purposes ....12.7 per cent.
County purposes ....31.3 per cent.
City purposes ....13.1 per cent.
Township purposes ....10.6 per cent.
School purposes ....32.3 per cent.

100 per cent.

This brings to light some interesting facts. The most striking is the heavy outlay for education. Whereas it is shown in the table of state outlay above that the state annually expends about three times as much for penal and charitable work as for higher education, yet, when the local divisions are considered, as they should be, the fact is apparent that for educational purposes alone these spend annually about three times as much as the entire state outlay, for all purposes whatsoever. This applies to all moneys which are raised through the channels of taxation. But it is also true if we include state income from fees, etc., for these are more than offset by the income of the permanent school fund.

The objects of county outlay do not appear in the table. They are chiefly the county administrative government, the judiciary, county buildings, such as court house and jail, and county bridges and poor farms. City governments in Kansas play a much less important part than the county governments, since the cities of the state are all small. The chief outlay here is, in general, for the administration of the city government, the judiciary and police, city halls and jails, and in many instances, for the public utilities, water and light. Special improvements such as paving, sewerage, etc., constitute irregular expenditures, and are met by special assessment.

The township outlay is the least of all, since this local division has very few and simple functions. The chief objects of outlay here are roads, bridges, and a few administrative officers.

These findings give a picture of an average, or rather a *composite* citizen, who happens to pay exactly $100 a year in taxes, and for the following purposes, in the order of their importance:

For schools	$32 30
For county purposes	31 30
For city purposes	13 10
For state purposes	12 70
For township purposes	10 60
All purposes	$100 00

This shows the true relations between the kinds of taxes paid. Another basis is necessary to show actual amounts of taxes paid. The average annual tax in Kansas for all purposes is now $14,700,000, or $10 per capita, or 4.2 per cent. of assessed valuation.[1]

Therefore, the actual taxes paid for each individual in the state, and the purposes of these taxes, are the following:

For schools	$3 23
For county purposes	3 13
For city purposes	1 31
For state purposes	1 27
For township purposes	1 06
All purposes	$10 00

Considering this tax levy as a true index of the outlay in each case, a method correct for Kansas, the relative importance is shown of each division of government, from the state down.

A comparison of municipal, state and federal debt is shown in Appendix E.

---

[1] Compare with United States:

	1901	1902	1903
Total expenditures	$621,598,546	$593,038,903	$640,323,450
Per capita expenditures	$8 01	$7 51	$7 97
Total receipts	$699,316,531	$684,326,280	$694,621,118
Per capita receipts	$9 01	$8 66	$8 64

The matter of small leaks in the state outlay was mentioned as something overlooked in the popular clamor for rigid economy. These drains, small in detail, aggregate in a few years thousands of dollars of absolute waste. They come principally from that pernicious incubus of our political system whereby successful candidates are supposed to distribute patronage to their "friends." A small brood thus batten at the public crib from year to year. An example of this may be cited. Transcribing the journals of the House and Senate and filing a manuscript copy of the same was a budget item for several years, representing an outlay of from $1,000 to $3,000 per session for the annual sessions then held. Later this duty was performed equally well by officers already appointed—the chief clerk of the House, and the secretary of the Senate—at a total outlay of $800, thus saving the state about $1,000 a year. In 1884 this transcribing cost but $250.

At the present time duties and services are multiplied to an absurd extent, and many cases as unsavory as the above are familiar to all who take the care to observe.

The state has made outlays of money from the beginning which partake more of the nature of investments than mere expenditures. These are for the erection and repair of public buildings. The total cost of these to the state is shown in the table below:

COST OF STATE BUILDINGS, 1861–1902

Penitentiary	$1,400,292
Capitol	3,044,853
Reformatory institutions[2]	557,194
Higher educational institutions[3]	893,912
State charitable institutions[4]	800,483

These figures include money spent for permanent repairs, as well as original cost of erection. In cases of bond issues—as with

---

[2] Boys' Reform School, Topeka.
Girls' Industrial School, Beloit.
Hutchinson Reformatory [Boys], Hutchinson.
[3] State University, Lawrence.
Normal School, Emporia.
Agricultural College, Manhattan.
[4] Insane Asylums, Topeka, Osawatomie, Parsons.
Deaf and Dumb Asylum, Olathe.
Blind School, Kansas City.
Imbecile Asylum, Winfield.

the capitol and the penitentiary—the interest on these bonds, and the discount as well, are included in the cost account, for these represent actual outlay to the state. The interest on the $320,000 of capitol bonds, for instance, was $672,000. Cost of maintenance from year to year is not included. The present value of this state property is shown in Appendix I.

Another interesting group of state expenditures is presented in the following table:

MISCELLANEOUS OUTLAY, 1861–1902

State printing	$2,232,804 04
Subsidies to private industries (beet sugar)	99,936 50
Subsidies to private charities	154,425 00
County destitute insane	729,811 00

The state early adopted the county asylum system for the care of all ordinary cases of pauperism. As overseers of the poor, the mayor and council in incorporated cities, and the trustees of the civil townships have certain wide powers in granting outside relief. The larger counties are now employing a commissioner of the poor for the old, loose system seemed to promote pauperism, rather than cure it. The tendency under the system is to limit relief almost wholly to those who are actual inmates of the county poor houses in rural communities, and to those in cities who perform some work test. The only outside relief granted regularly by the state is that made for the county destitute insane for whom there is no room in the state institutions. This varies from a few thousand dollars to a hundred thousand dollars a year, as the legislature may see fit. This outlay, however, is expected to disappear from the budget with the increase in the capacity of the state institutions.

A comparison of state outlay for charities with the county outlay shows the following interesting figures:

STATE AND LOCAL CHARITIES.[5]

STATE CHARITABLE INSTITUTIONS.		
maintenance for year ending June, 1899	$462,840 49	
per capita cost		.324
COUNTY CHARITIES.		
outlay on asylum farms	$135,978 40	
outside relief	209,152 67	$345,131 07
per capita cost		.212
Total per capita cost		$ .566

[5] 15 *Bureau of Labor*, 1899, pt. vi.

Hence it is evident that the burden is about equal for state and local charities. The state outlay, however, is a matter of public interest and public scrutiny, and therefore follows some scientific and accredited principles, whereas the local outlay is in accordance with no principle. Not infrequently it does as much harm as good by nursing dependence and pauperism.

Income.—An examination of state income will now be made, with special reference to the source of that income. The general property tax is, of course, the principal source. To this it is necessary to give attention in detail in a later paragraph. The other sources of income now employed by the state are fees, interest on permanent funds, state industries and gifts.

The fee system is very extensive, especially in the smaller local divisions. In certain offices, where the service is light and only occasional, fees are used. As the constancy and regularity of the work increase, the salary increases and fees, as a rule disappear. These fees are regulated by law and vary according to the nature of the service.

The General Statutes of 1901 shows a list of fees of the following classes and kinds: bank examiner; supreme court clerk; marshal; stenographer; corporation charter; foreign building and loan associations; examination in dentistry; public stock yards; sanitary commission; assistants and clerks of secretary of state; sealers of weights and measures; superintendent of insurance; inspector of oils; inspector of grains; game warden. These are all state fees. The list of fee payments might be extended to include those in connection with city courts, assignment proceedings, etc. The list for the other local divisions includes fees paid for services of treasurers, clerks, sheriffs, attorneys, registrars of deeds, jurors, witnesses, coroners, notaries public, justices of the peace, probate judges, surveyors, commissioners, arbitrators and umpires, superintendents of bridges, appraisers, and fence viewers.

The fees of chief fiscal importance to the state are those of the bank commissioner and the superintendent of insurance, for in these two cases the fees are more than adequate for the support of the departments. This is one step, at least, in the direction of a complete segregation of the sources of local and state revenue. Its wisdom and success will doubtless lead to further advance in the same direction.

The interest income of the state comes from the permanent school funds, and must be applied without fail to the annual expenses of the different schools. These funds aggregate about $7,000,000 and are invested for the most part at 7 per cent. in school district bonds. They therefore yield the state about half a million dollars a year. This is chiefly for the benefit of the common schools, as the institutions of higher education depend on legislative appropriations for support. In 1900 these funds were invested, or uninvested, as follows:

```
Permanent school fund, invested.................... $6,643,297 44
Permanent school fund, uninvested....................    63,650 24
University permanent fund, invested..................   148,260 82
Universty permanent fund, uninvested.................       969 17
Normal school permanent fund, invested..............    200,919 01
Normal school permanent fund, uninvested............      3,725 05
```

These funds, however, contribute but a small part of the money necessary for the maintenance of the state school system. Even in the case of the common schools, where the permanent fund is almost $7,000,000, about seven-eighths of the support comes from taxation, (See Appendix B.).

Of the state industries, little need be said here. They are not intended as a source of income to the state, but were created for other purposes. A few small and fiscally unimportant industries are conducted at the state charitable and reformatory institutions. The state prison with its thousand convicts is the seat of the most important industrial work of the commonwealth. Coal is mined in a state mine by the prisoners, and furnished to the different state institutions, to meet all their needs. They give a paper credit of $2 a ton, merely to facilitate proper account keeping. This means a great annual savings to the state. A brick plant is also operated here, likewise to supply public institutions. Seventy-five to eighty prisoners are employed in the operation of the binder twine plant installed a few years ago. The output of this plant is sold and the cash turned into the state treasury. In this industry there is no competition with the free labor of the state, and a ready market

is always close at hand. The labor is beneficial to the prisoners
and a source of profit to the state. The prison is practically
self-supporting, outside of special appropriations for new buildings, etc.

These incomes described above are all in the nature of regular
incomes. There are also certain irregular incomes which must
be mentioned. First, and most important, is the matter of
loans, made to meet the exigencies of the times. The importance
of this has been illustrated in the foregoing pages of this history. As the state wealth increases, however, less and less re-
liance is placed on this extraordinary source of income, and
more expenditures are provided for by the regular, annual income.

A little over 100,000 acres of public school lands yet remain
unsold, and the proceeds of this will go to augment the school
fund. The federal government still holds about 1,000,000 acres
of land in the state, and as this is sold to settlers, 5 per cent. of
the proceeds will be added to the permanent school fund. These
two streams of revenue will in the end increase this fund by
some $500,000, and since, by law, this fund can never be di-
minished, its future of usefulness is to be a very long one.

A final source of income to the state is that of gifts. These
are chiefly in the nature of donations of buildings to her educational institutions, such as the Spooner Library and the
Fowler Shops to the State University, or of scientific gifts to
the state at large. In this class are the Goss Ornithological
Collection, now kept at the State Capitol, and the Stormont
Medical Library. The "conscience fund" must complete this
list, unimportant fiscally, but very interesting as a commentary
on human nature. In 1900 the sum of $24.83 was returned to
the state under this head.

To appreciate the importance of these different sources of
revenue, it is necessary to examine concrete cases. There is
therefore presented below a full table of receipts for the years
1901 and 1902, showing both the source and amount:

RECEIPTS, 1901 AND 1902

Source.	1901.	1902.
Direct taxes..	$1,815,789	$1,914,556
Fees..		
Oil inspector....................	19,984	19,550
Auditor....	1,654	1,469
Secretary of state....	9,133	12,896
Courts....	11,258	14,133
Bank commissioner..........	8,351	8,689
Grain inspector..	38,403	34,206
Medical examinations.................................	....	12,521
Stenographers.	2,061	2,715
Live stock sanitary commission..	2,622	4,260
Superintendent of insurance........................	31,807	47,041
United States government......	35,085	42,382
Penitentiary and other institutions..............	29,258	106,515
Accretions to annual and per. school funds through sales, rents, interest, balances, etc.	644,409	630,108
Balance in treasury............................. ..	510,711	577,626
Miscellaneous, funds, etc.............................	1,044,132	729,340
Totals.........	$4,204,657	$4,158,007

The last three items in the receipts above, it should be borne
in mind, are of the nature of balances, principally, in the
various funds, and when subtracted from the total income leave
some $2,000,000 as the real annual income of the state. This
amount, the table clearly shows, comes almost entirely from
direct taxes. And hence it is true, as already assumed, that the
income from direct taxes is a fair index of outlay for the various
objects of public support, such as schools, municipal and state
government, etc.

Municipalities employ certain sources of revenue in addition
to those used by the state, and discussed above. Chief among
these is the license or occupation tax, similar to those in vogue
in southern cities. Newton, for instance, a city of the second
class, in 1882 levied a business license on more than twenty
kinds of business, ranging from $40 a day on circuses and
menageries, to $5 a year on merchants with a stock of goods not
exceeding $1,000 worth. This city ordinance stood the test of
the Kansas Supreme Court.[6] The constitutional provision of
uniformity applies only to taxes, not to licenses, privilege fees,
or franchise fees.

The road tax of $3 is a local tax which seems to yield a min-
imum of good, from whatever point considered. Able-bodied

---

[6] 29 *Kans.*, 364.

men, from twenty-one to forty-five years old, pay this tax, either in money, or labor at $1.50 per day. Three dollars a day is allowed for a man and team. As a reminder of civic duties, this tax is a success, but as an experiment in road building it is a pronounced failure.

For paving the streets and other special work of this kind in cities, a special assessment is made on the property benefited by the improvement. In a growing city these assessments frequently prove very onerous to those who happen to be owners of abutting property where the improvement is located.

The poll tax still figures in the Kansas financial system, but is playing a constantly decreasing part. Cities of the second and third classes are authorized to use it, but rarely resort to it. A law in 1899 authorized townships in sparsely settled counties to maintain fire-guards to prevent the spread of prairie fires, and to have the poll tax paid by work on these guards.

Taxation.—We are now ready to examine the main features of taxation, for this, as we have seen, is first and foremost in importance as a source of revenue. To give the discussion a logical sequence, consideration will first be had of the assessment of property, and then the levy and collection of taxes, and finally some observations will be made on the merits of the system.

Property is grouped in two general classes, real and personal, and the aim of assessment is to assess all real and personal property in the state once, unless it is expressly exempt. The statute defines real property as "the land itsef * * * and all buildings, fixtures, improvements, mines, minerals, quarries, mineral springs and wells, rights and privileges appertaining thereto." The term personal property, according to the law "shall include every tangible thing which is the subject of ownership, not forming part and parcel of real property; also all tax sale certificates, judgments, notes, bonds and mortgages, and all evidences of debt secured by lien on real estate; also the capital stock, undivided profits, and all other assets of every company, incorporated or unincorporated, and every share or interest in such stock, profits, or assets by whatever name the same may be designated."

The constitution provides for certain classes of exemptions, and these are elaborated somewhat in the statutes. The list changes from decade to decade, constantly growing larger, as new kinds of property claim the right of exemption. It was originally intended for property of a purely public or social nature, and for the small amount of $200 of personalty for each family. This last provision looks innocent enough and incapable of abuse, but such is not the case. Assessors juggle with it. Some families divide ownership of their property in such a way that this exemption is made to apply three or four times in a single family. Its commonest abuse is in subtracting it from the completed assessment which is made on a basis of one-fourth or one-fifth real values. This swells the $200 exemption to $800 or $1,000, whereas it should have been subtracted from actual values, before assessment is completed.

The other exemptions now provided by law are as follows:[7]

(1) All school houses and church buildings, with the land owned by each, up to ten acres, provided it is not leased or used for profit, and also the parsonage of any church with its land up to one-half acre.

(2) Graveyards.

(3) All buildings and equipment of scientific, literary and benevolent associations, used exclusively for scientific, literary and benevolent purposes, together with the lands occupied by each, up to five acres, if not leased or used for profit.

(4) All moneys and credits belonging exclusively to universities, colleges, academies, or public schools of any kind, or to religious, literary, scientific or benevolent and charitable institutions, not exceeding in amounts the charter provisions in each case.

(5) All property of the state or of the United States.

(6) All property belonging to any county, city, town, or school district, except land bid off for counties at tax sales.

(7) The wearing apparel of every person.

(8) All public libraries.

(9) Family libraries and school books of every person and family, not exceeding in any one case the value of $50.

---

[7] *Gen'l. Statutes,* 1901, ch. 107.

(10) All memorial halls owned by the Grand Army of the Republic, and land in each case up to one-half acre.

These constitute all the positive exemptions at present contemplated by the statute. For the benefit of debtors who are fortunate enough to be creditors at the same time, provision is made that debts owing in good faith may be deducted from gross amount of credits due. Every person is supposed to list all money in his possession, and all credits due or to become due him.

These are the general rules of assessment, and the machinery for carrying them out is very simple. It is the local assessors. In cities of the first and second class, the mayor and council appoint the assessors annually; in the county the township trustee is the local assessor, elected yearly.

But for the government of this assessment machinery, the regulations are intricate and complex. In other words, the attempt is made to assess all property uniformly and equitably, and the attempt fails. The law declares in plain terms that these men shall assess all property at its true value in money. They are bound by an oath to do this, and the property owner likewise may be required by the assessor to verify his returns with an oath. The law is plain on this point, 100 per cent. is the true basis of valuation contemplated. Another provision is made, which on its face, looks like a very wise one. Before the assessors begin their work in the spring, they are to meet together at the county seat and there agree upon an "equal basis of valuation." In other words, they are to decide what 100 per cent. of the actual value is, when applied to a horse, a cow, a wagon, an acre of land, etc. But this law is flagrantly violated year after year. No better evidence of this is needed than the official minutes of these annual assessors' meetings. A few cases are cited here from the 1897 reports, for illustrations:[8]

---

[8] 13 *Bureau of Labor*, 1897, p. 14.

BASIS OF ASSESSMENT OF REAL AND PERSONAL PROPERTY FOR 1897, AS
AGREED UPON OFFICIALLY BY TOWNSHIP AND CITY ASSESSORS.

County.	Realty.	Personalty.
	Per cent.	Per cent.
Atchison	25	25
Chase	50	33⅓
Cherokee	33⅓	50
Decatur	100	100
Gove	200	33⅓
McPherson	40	40
Rawlins	100	100
Republic	20	33⅓
Sedgwick	30	30
Wabaunsee	20	33⅓
Woodson	50	50

An investigator, reporting this method of assessment to the
Bureau of Labor, speaks of it in these terms.[9] "Most astound-
ing is it to read the official minutes of the meetings of county
boards of assessors in the spring of 1898. In advance of assessment these boards met together to decide whether they would
follow the whole state law, which expressly commands the assessment of all property at its full cash value, or whether they
would obey one-third the law, that is, assess property at one-
third of its value; or whether they would only obey one-fifth of
the law. The writer attended the meeting of one board, where
assessors openly stated that they would not pledge themselves
to assess at any fixed ratio, as they knew that some of the assessors present would assess it a less ratio than that which was
adopted, whatever that might be. Harmony was finally at-
tained by the passage of a resolution to assess at the usual ratio,
and a general laugh followed the inquiry by one innocent member as to what that ratio was. No one seemed able to answer."

The minutes of Cherokee county are equally interesting.[10]
They read: "On motion, it was agreed to assess all property
at its actual value, but after much discussion the motion was re-
considered, and the following substitute chosen:

"Resolved, That it is the sense of this body that in future
years all property should be assessed at its actual cash value.

"On motion it was agreed to assess all personal property *
* * at 50 per cent. of its actual value.

---

[9] 13 *Bureau of Labor,* p. 76.
[10] 13 *Bureau of Labor,* p. 58.

"On motion it was agreed to assess all real estate at one-third its actual value."

It must be conceded that these assessors were at least capable of giving good advice for the future, even if they did not follow it themselves.

Thus from county to county the agreed basis of valuation fluctuates. To illustrate the nature of the statement or list of property commonly dealt with by the assessors, and to give another concrete example of astonishing valuations, the schedule of Dickinson county for 1898 is presented.[11]

"Horses, 6 months old, and under 1 year...................... $5 to $10
Horses, 1 year old, and under 2 years......................... $5 to $15
Horses, 2 years old, and under 3 years........................$10 to $25
Horses, 3 years old, and over 3 years......................... $5 to $40
Mules and asses, 6 months old and over, same as horses.
Stallions for service, 12 times fee.
Jacks for service, same as horses.
Neat cattle, 6 months old and under 1 year.................... $8 to $12
Neat cattle, 1 year old and under 2 years....................$12 to $20
Neat cattle, 2 years old and under 3 years...................$15 to $25
Neat cattle, 3 years old and over............................$15 to $40
Fat cattle, per pound..3½ to 4 cts.
Sheep, 6 months old and over................................. $2.50
Hogs, per cwt... $2.50
Farm implements, threshing machines, engines, horsepowers,
    wagons and pleasure carriages, gold and silver and other
    watches, at judgment of assessor.
Pianofortes ....$50 to $150
Other musical instruments at judgment of assessor.
Wheat, per bushel... 40 to 60 cts.
Corn, per bushel .... 12 cents
Rye, per bushel... 20 cents.
Oats, per bushel .... 12 cents.
Kaffeir corn, per bushel.................................... 12 cents.
Sorghum, per bushel .... 15 cents.
All other items, judgment of assessor.
"On motion it was voted to deduct the constitutional exemption ($200) from full value on personal property, and divide the remainder by 3.
"On motion, real estate to be assessed at one-fourth its actual value."

These minutes suggest in a very forcible manner what sort of uniformity of assessment is reached throughout the state. This is certainly a queer way of reaching the "uniform and equal rate of assessment and taxation" contemplated by the constitution.

---

[11] 13 *Bureau of Labor,* p. 60.

Speaking of these minutes given above, and others of like tenor, a citizen of Kansas very tersely said; "Summed up, a system that will permit a cow to cross an imaginary line and double or treble her value, or that will allow a bushel of wheat, if it happens to be in the next county on the first day of March, to shrink in value one-half, one-fourth, or have no value at all, and treats all other property in the same way, or that encourages the use of the exemption laws as shown above, should be immediately remedied or abolished, or failing to do either, the age limit for 'mules and asses' as enumerated in the above schedules, should be extended to include the citizen and voter, and count us all in where we belong."[12]

Enough has been said to indicate the true character of the work undertaken by the assessors, and to show that they adjourn from their preliminary meeting with the deliberate intention of disregarding the first law enacted for their guidance. There are various other regulations, better obeyed, which give them a working program. Some of these laws will now be examined, together with the result of their operation. The general statute now has separate and distinct provisions for real estate, personal property, railways, banks and bankers, merchants and manufacturers, and telegraph and telephone companies. For our present purpose it is best to examine briefly the assessment of the first two general classes,—realty and personalty,—and then the separate classes differentiated from these.

The listing and valuation of real estate falls to the assessor, fortunately, but once in two years, and not annually as is the case with personal property. He is to view the land in question, examine the improvements, and lump all together. Returns are to be made in full to the county clerks by May 10. A strong oath is provided for the assessor as a final goad to honesty. Iron-clad oaths are also provided in the case of personal property to ensure the accuracy of the annual returns.

The great crying evil of assessment as applied today is its

---

[12] 13 *Bureau of Labor*, pt. I.

inequality. Under-assessment is of course the rule. But this rule does not work uniformly, and hence inequalities do not tend to become leveled down. Flagrant violations of uniformity appear as between individuals, between localities, and between classes of property. The general omnipresent evil of under-assessment is graphically represented in the diagram below:

PLATE I.—RELATION OF ASSESSED VALUATION TO TRUE VALUATION, 1860–1890

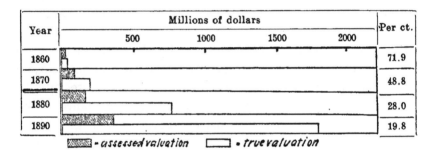

True valuations are taken from the United States census reports, and the assessed valuations are those returned by county clerks to the state auditor.

Since more and more property escapes assessment and taxation as shown above,—28.1 per cent. in 1860, 80.7 per cent. in 1890,—the question presents itself, what class of property is it that escapes? The answer is, the larger the property, the smaller is its rate of assessment. The truth of this statement is illustrated in the authentic table below:

ASSESSMENT RATES ON SMALL PROPERTIES, LARGE PROPERTIES, AND OTHER CLASSES OF PROPERTY.[13]

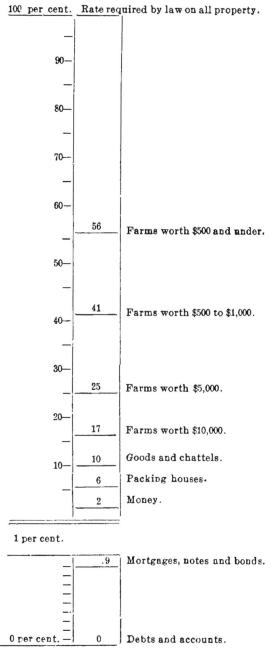

100 per cent. Rate required by law on all property.

90—

80—

70—

60—

56 —— Farms worth $500 and under.

50—

41 —— Farms worth $500 to $1,000.

40—

30—

25 — Farms worth $5,000.

20—

17 — Farms worth $10,000.

10 — Goods and chattels.

10—

6 | Packing houses.

2 | Money.

1 per cent.

.9 | Mortgages, notes and bonds.

0 per cent. — 0 | Debts and accounts.

[13] The sources of this table make it of peculiar value. It is based (a) on actual sales of real estate; 1,648 sales in 30 counties (13 *Bureau of Labor*, pt. I,

When once the assessor has broken away from the law regulating his conduct and requiring the 100-per cent. basis of valuation, he has no longer any guiding principles, except such considerations as come up in each individual case of assessment. A small holding he accordingly assesses at something like its real value; but in the case of a large holding, he is willing to knock off a few thousands, since this still leaves a large sum. But should he reduce the value of a small holding even a few hundred, there would be nothing left. Then there is another factor of some importance, namely, the prestige and general influence of the person with the large holding. He is more likely to be favored with a lenient assessment, than is his humble neighbor. These things partly explain the great disparities seen in the table above.

Inequalities between persons in the same county are overwhelmingly numerous. Only a few instances will be given here, but they could be multiplied almost without limit. In Saline county two 160-acre farms were sold, one for $5,000, the other for $1,000. The assessment on them the same year was, respectively, $600 and $500. In Cowley county, the same year, one farm sold for $800, another for $2,400. Both were assessed at $200.[14] In these cases, *bona fide* sales were made, a fact which strongly emphasizes this evil of inequality between individuals. We may add two cases from Douglas county, where the true value was set by appraisers of probated estate. In case number one, household goods were appraised at $128, but assessed at $215, or 168 per cent. of true value. In case number two, goods and chattels were appraised at $56,000, but assessed at $275, that is, one-half of one per cent. of true value.[15] These cases are typical and must stand for that wide and general class of individual inequalities which is one curse of the present assessment system.

1897); and (b) on probated estates as follows: Goods and chattels, 247 estates in 9 counties; notes and mortgages, 115 estates in 7 counties; debts and accounts, 34 estates in 4 counties; money, 134 estates in 8 counties; (14 *Bureau of Labor*, p. 8, ff.); (c) packing house returns of capital invested, as reported in 13 *Bureau of Labor*, pt. I.

[14] 9 *Bureau of Labor*, p. 718.
[15] 14 *Bureau of Labor*, p. 30.

A third class of inequalities is that between different localities. The preparation of the assessors at their preliminary county meeting where the "basis of valuation" is settled, makes this follow as a necessary result. Evils here are most prevalent of all, but only a few typical cases can be cited at this point. In the year 1901, for example, horses were assessed as low as $1 in one county, and as high as $150 in another. The minimum assessment of cattle varied from $1 to $15; gold watches from $1 to $100; pianos from $5 to $500. Other personal property was assessed in most counties at one-third its real value; in McPherson county at 20 per cent.; in Reno, adjoining this county, at 100 per cent., and in other counties "at the discretion of the assessor."[16] In some counties grain in store was not assessed at all, but was entirely ignored by the township assessors. In many counties household furniture of all kinds,—plate, jewelry, musical instruments, etc.,—was lumped at from $20 to $50 per family, regardless of the amount or quality of the same.

So on the whole, therefore, there seems no room for even a hope of justice as between different localities.

There are yet other evils inherent in the system. The charge of double taxation is one of the commonest. It comes in many forms. To the farmer it is a concrete evil. Farmer A, for instance, owns a cow worth $50, on which he pays taxes. Next year Farmer B buys this cow at a public sale, giving in exchange his note at one year for $50. There is still the one piece of productive property—the cow—worth $50, but if the assessor does his duty, he finds and lists $100 worth of property, that is, A $50 on the note and B $50 on the cow. Where he found $50 the year before, he now finds $100. The temptation to violate the law here is very strong, too strong, in fact, for the average citizen. But the table given on a preceding page shows that nine-tenths of one per cent. of notes are taxed; that is, nine out of a thousand.

Assessment of mortgages is open to the same objection among holders of encumbered estates. Two men seem to be taxed on the same piece of property when both land and mortgage are taxed at their full value. The situs of the mortgage is declared

[16] *Report of Kans. State Tax Comm.*, 1901, p. 10.

to be the owner's residence.[17]   Should he happen to hold a mortgage on land 'in some state like California, considering the mortgage a part interest in the real estate, he would be taxed twice on the mortgage, according to law.   But, as a matter of fact, mortgages, as well as notes, practically exempt themselves from taxation entirely.   They produce no revenue to the state or municipalities, but their continuance on the taxable list of the statutes doubtless serves to maintain their interest rates at a somewhat higher level than the normal.

With money, about the same thing is true at present.   The assessor is supposed to find it all.   But on the first day of March, 1901, when the bank deposits, alone, aside from all moneys outside, amounted to over $70,000,000, the Kansas assessors were only able to find $3,059,424.[18]

These evils of under-listing and non-listing cannot be entirely grouped under the old-fashioned sin of dishonesty.   There is an element of self-defence in it.   Each knows the prevailing custom, and must defend himself accordingly.   Love of fair play, it 'is highly possible, would ensure a cheerful listing of all the property of an individual, did he feel any assurance that his neighbors too were being assessed at full values.

Assessment of the coal mines of the state follows the caprice of the local assessors, but is usually at a small fraction of the capital actually invested.

The assessor's directions for assessing merchants and manufacturers are very meager.   He simply takes their statement of the average value of stock on hand during the year.   Banks and bankers are reached by assessing the capital stock and surplus at the bank, regardless of where stockholders may live.

For the assessment of corporations a few special regulations have been differentiated from the general mass of tax laws. Railroads, sleeping car companies, telegraph and telephone companies, have now been taken out of the hands of local assessors, and given to state boards.   Express companies are still subject to the crude, primitive method of local assessment.

The assessment of railroads is made annually by the state

---

[17] 5 *Kan. A.*, 90.
[18] *Report of Kans. State Tax Comm.*, 1901, p. 10.

board of five men,—lieutenant-governor, secretary of state, treasurer, auditor, and attorney-general. Real estate not connected with the track, however, is assessed locally, the same as other real estate. But that which constitutes the right-of-way, depot grounds, etc., comes within the purview of the state board. In making the annual assessment of railroads, this board proceeds with two things in view, namely, the value of the fixed plant, and the value of the rolling stock, both of which are considered as personal property.[19] The guiding principle seems to be the cost of construction, checked up against the cost of reproduction. Minutes of the state board bear out this idea. No serious effort is made to reach the franchise value, although the impression is growing that this can be no longer neglected with indifference. It is interesting to follow a case of assessment by this board. According to law, the board meets on the third Monday in April, and has before it for consideration the sworn statements sent in by the railroads of the state. The law provides that this statement shall set forth;

(1) the statistics of right-of-way, track and road-bed, length of main track in Kansas and its total length, its proportion in each city, township, and county.

(2) length, location, etc., of side tracks.

(3) complete list of location, value, etc., of depots, station-houses, water stations and all other buildings.

(4) number of ties in track per mile; weight of iron or steel rails per yard used in main or side tracks; what joints or chairs are used in track; the ballasting of road, whether with gravel or dirt; the length of time iron has been used, and length of time road has been built.

(5) full value of rolling stock. This list shall distinctly set forth the number, class and value of all locomotives, passenger cars, sleeping cars, dining cars, wrecking cars, pay cars, and all other kinds of cars owned or leased by said company.

(6) (a) The amount of capital stock authorized and number of shares into which such stock is divided; (b) amount of capital stock paid up; (c) market value of such stock. If no market value, then actual value.

---

[19] 9 *Kan. A.*, 545.

(7) A detailed inventory of all tools, repair materials, **and** all other personal property.

These are the facts in the order which the law states, and these constitute the working data of the board. The only expert testimony heard by the board is that of the attorneys and tax agents of the roads who appear and seek reduction in their valuations.

The board after more or less deliberation fixes upon the value of the rolling stock. In the minutes of one meeting, for instance, it is said that by "personal inspection" they arrived at the following valuations:[20] locomotives, cost new $7,500, assessed at $2,500; sleeping cars, cost $16,000, assessed $6,000; dining cars, cost $11,000, assessed $4,000; pay cars, cost $4,000, assessed $1,500; and so on down the entire list of rolling stock to "rubble and push cars,"—cost $30, assessed $10. The board that fixed these values next proceeded by "unanimous vote" to assess the fixed plant of several roads, by assessments varying from $2,000 to $7,500 per mile. After having assessed the Santa Fé, Union Pacific and some of the other most important roads of the state, the board fell into a thoughtful mood and devoted one whole meeting to the question of a proper basis for assessing right-of-way, road bed, trackage, etc. "The value of a line of railroad," declared the board, "is not easy to determine. The most potential factors in determining such value may be named as follows." Here the board laid down a series of seven propositions, the last of which is a blanket provision including all the rest. The seven factors are

(1) actual cost of road ready for use,
(2) business afforded by country along the road,
(3) business done by road, considering competition,
(4) cost of operation,
(5) terminal facility advantages,
(6) whether a trunk line or feeder of a trunk line,
(7) "What is actual value of road today?"

This illustrates the gropings of the board after some true test of faculty or ability of the roads to pay taxes. The quest

---

[20] *Assessment of R. R. Property, etc.* Pamphlet. Topeka, 1891.

is rather a baffling one thus far. Aside from these data, the board has access to the reports of gross and net earnings so far as these are returned to the state board of railroad commissioners. But some roads refuse to make these returns, and others use book-keeping which is more misleading than enlightening. So the board of assessors scarcely hope to attain more than a rough justice. Considering all methods of assessment thus far observed, the conclusion seems warranted that railroads are assessed low, but not so low as other forms of property.

It is a matter of belief, based on common observation, that personal property in a community as old as Kansas, should be at least equal in value to the real property. But personal property and railroads are falling so far behind real estate in the assessment returns that Kansas seems rapidly tending towards a single tax on land and land-improvements.

The situation is accurately exhibited in the interesting diagram following:

PLATE II.—ASSESSMENT OF REAL ESTATE, PERSONAL PROPERTY, AND RAIL-
ROADS.

Showing increase in assessment of real estate, relatively and absolutely,
from 1873 to 1902.

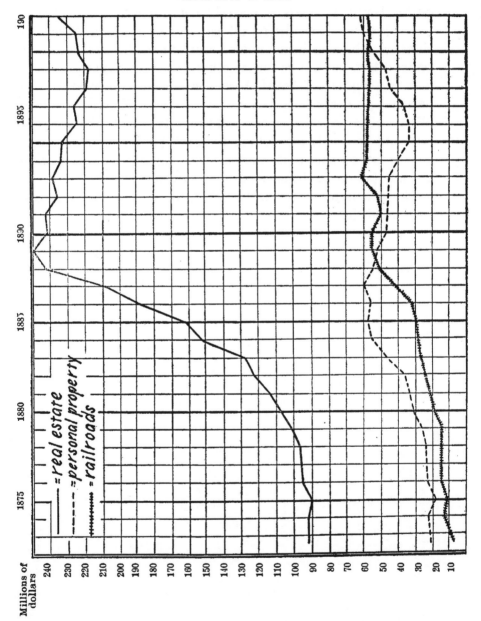

Prior to 1873 railroads were not separated from other personal property in the assessment returns, and hence the table begins at that year.

The state board of railroad assessors has also within the purview of its authority the assessment of Pullman and other sleeping cars. The board of railroad commissioners require full reports covering capital stock, cost of equipment, gross earnings, operating expenses, dividends declared, miles run in Kansas, and total mileage. "Miles traveled" is the basis of the proportion used in determining the value of the equipment assignable to Kansas. Since these cars make regular trips, it is easy to determine what proportion of their run is within the limits of Kansas and what proportion elsewhere. Each car is usually assessed at from $4,000 to $6,000. If half its run is in Kansas, then half the value of the car is considered taxable in Kansas. These cars yielded a tax in 1902 of $8,655.19.[21] The same year this company paid a total tax in Michigan of $6.45.[22] This beggarly amount was due to a defect in the wording of the law, by which the technical rights of interstate commerce were trenched upon.[23]

The railroad companies using the Pullman cars are held liable for the tax on them. The law for assessing Pullman cars provides that the proper persons shall list "all sleeping cars, dining cars, palace or other cars that make *regular* trips over any railroad in this state, and not owned by such railroad company." By the wording of this statute, it is evident, that cars not used *regularly*, such as refrigerator and fruit cars, escape assessment and taxation altogether. And this is becoming an item of considerable importance.

In the assessment of express companies the gross error is still embraced of ignoring the unity of this class of property. Each individual horse, wagon, and pouch is assessed as though it were a separate and independent piece of property used wholly for local purposes. And this is done in spite of the fact that the Supreme Court has made contrary rulings in the case of

[21] 17 *R. R. Comm. Report.*
[22] 2 *Report, Board of State Tax Comm.*, Michigan, p. 78-9.
[23] *Fargo vs. Michigan*, 121 *U. S.*, 230.

railroads, telegraph companies, sleeping car companies, and lastly, in the case of express companies themselves. The famous case of this kind is that of the *Adams Express Company vs. Ohio State Auditor*,[24] in which Chief Justice Fuller renders an opinion against the express company. One of the best pronouncements ever made on the subject of taxation, however, was that given by Justice Brewer on a rehearing of this case. Since this celebrated utterance applies to express companies in all the states the following words are quoted from it:

"Now, it is a cardinal rule which should never be forgotten that whatever property is worth for the purposes of income and sale, it is also worth for the purposes of taxation. * * * If a statute properly construed, contemplates only the taxation of horses and wagons, then those belonging to an express company, can be taxed at no higher value than those belonging to a farmer. But if the state comprehends all property in its scheme of taxation, then the good will of an organized and established industry must be recognized as a thing of value. The capital stock of a corporation and the shares in a joint stock company represent not only the tangible property but also the intangible, including therein all corporate franchises and contracts and good will of the concern.

"Now the same reality of its value of its intangible property exists when a company does not confine its work to the limits of a single State. Take for instance, the Adams Express Company. According to the returns filed by it with the auditor of the State of Ohio, as shown in the record of these cases, its number of shares was 120,000, the market value of each $140 to $150. Taking the smaller sum gives the value of the company's property taken as an entirety as $16,800,000. In other words, it is worth that for the purposes of income to the holders of the stock, and for the purposes of sale in the markets of the land. But in the same return, it shows that the value of its real estate owned in Ohio was only $25,170; of its real estate owned outside of Ohio, $3,005,157.52; or a total of $3,030,326.52; the value of its personal property in Ohio, $42,065; of personal property outside of Ohio, $1,117,426.05; or a total of $1,159,491.05;

---

[24] 165 *U. S.*, 194.

making a total valuation of its tangible property, $4,189,818.57, and upon that basis it insists that taxes shall be levied. But what a mockery of substantial justice it would be for a corporation whose property is worth to its stockholders for the purposes of income and sale, $16,800,000, to be adjudged liable for taxation on only one-fourth that amount. The value which property bears in the market, the amount for which its stock can be bought and sold, is the real value. Business men do not pay cash for property in moonshine or dreamland. They buy and pay for that which is of value in its power to produce income, or for purposes of sale.

"In conclusion, let us say, that this is eminently a practical age; that courts must recognize things as they are and as possessing a value which is accorded to them in the markets of the world, and that no fine-spun theories about situs should interfere to enable these large corporations whose business is carried on through many States, to escape from bearing in each State such a burden of taxation as a fair distribution of the actual value of their property among those States requires."

Pending this decision, some express companies were making strenuous efforts to escape taxation altogether. The United States Express Company, for example, filed with the Kansas board of railroad commissioners, a very brief report concerning its capital stock of $10,000,000, its mileage, etc., and concluded its statement with this interesting declaration: "This company has prepared this report, giving such information as it is able to give at this time, but it is given under protest, on the grounds that the business of the United States Express Company is interstate commerce and is regulated only by the Congress of the United States, and that the State of Kansas has no authority to exact reports concerning its business or to impose taxation on it thereunder." This statement is duly sworn to by the vice president of the United States Express company.[25] The personal property reported by this company in Kansas (it having no realty here) was $500; its mileage in Kansas one twenty-fifth of its total mileage, and its gross earnings for the

---

[25] 13 *Annual Report, Board R. R. Comm.*, p. 245.

state, $16,601.50. The tax on this $500 of personalty would
have amounted to some $20, and the attempt was even made to
dodge this. A distribution of the market value of this corporation, according to mileage, would have assigned to Kansas one
twenty-fifth of $10,000,000, or $400,000.

Under the Supreme Court decision there could not be a complete evasion of all taxes. But instead of applying the method
of valuation to these companies which Justice Brewer commended as fair, their assessment is left entirely to the local assessors. They assess a few horses, wagons, pouches and safes,
and a small amount of realty, with no consideration of their
income producing power as parts of a great business unity.
Thus the United States Express company in 1903 paid a few
dollars tax in Topeka (its principal Kansas office) on $365
worth of property, and a city license fee of $100. Or take the
1902 report of the Adams Express Company, for instance.[26]
They report a dividend of $8 a share on 120,000 shares, that
is, $960,000 for the year. They have no realty in Kansas and
only $3,040 worth of personalty. If their earnings are appor-
tioned to Kansas according to their mileage, then 1.48 per cent.
of the dividend, or $14,177 is due to the Kansas business.[27] This
would represent a net income on $3,040 of $14.177 in one year.
Since the state tax rate in 1902 was 5½ mills, then if this property were really assessed, as reported, at $3,040, this express
company paid to the state in taxes the municificent sum of
$16.72. State and local taxes together would swell the total
taxation on $3,040 to $133.76. This paltry figure is made somewhat larger by license fees charged in a few of the cities, but
in any event, it is absurdly low.

The American Express Company reports $6,973.87 worth of
personalty in Kansas, and no realty.[28] By their system of
bookkeeping they show $7,883.33 of gross earnings in the state,
and $20,993.53 of gross expenses. Yet they show no disposition
to quit the state.

The Pacific Express Company is the most extensive one in the

[26] 17 *Report, Board R. R. Comm.*, p. 69. ff.
[27] Total Railroad Mileage in U. S., 36,017 miles; Total Railroad Mileage in Kans., 532 miles.
[28] 17 *Rept., R. R. Comm.*, p. 70.

state, having one-sixth of its total railroad mileage here. They report dividends in 1902 of 13½ per cent. on the common stock, or $810,000 of dividends. The value of their tangible property in the state does not appear in their report. One-sixth of their market value, however, is $1,000,000, counting the stock at par. But the present method of assessment can take no cognizance of this. In Topeka, where their largest office in the state is located, tax is paid on a $600 assessment. This includes a building on leased land.[29]

The Wells Fargo Express Company has about the same mileage in Kansas as the Pacific, but it constitutes only about one-tenth of their total mileage. They are capitalized at $8,000,000. They report dividends of 8 per cent. for 1902, or $640,000. In the matter of unintelligible reporting, they easily take the lead. Under "operating expenses" we find these items:[30]

> "Salaries of general officers........................ $201,900 00
> Stationery and printing........................... 6,852,670 81
> Stationery and printing, general offices............ 120,467 75"

Aside from their license fee of $100, they paid taxes in Topeka in 1903 on an assessment of $1,855 of realty and personalty.

A great part of the business of these five express companies is transacted through the hundreds of depot offices in the small towns and villages of the state, without the expense to the companies of maintaining separate offices and buildings. In these cases, of course, there is practically no tangible property to assess. Surely the public welfare demands that these companies be subject to assessment by a state board.

All telegraph and telephone companies with wires crossing county lines come under the authority of the state board of telegraph and telephone assessors. The constitution of this board is identical with the board of railroad assessors, but it meets one week earlier in April of each year. Detailed reports are called for from the various telegraph and telephone companies of the state, and these companies are also given a hearing before the board. They regularly ask for a reduction over the preceding

---

[29] Private letter of County Treasurer of Shawnee county, Kans., Feb. 2, 1904.
[30] 17 *Rept., R. R. Comm.*

year's assessment. The board makes "construction and business" of each plant the basis of valuation. Franchises are not considered, but the board fixes the value of this property by comparison with the valuation of other personal property within the state.[31]

Assessment of street cars is still in the dark ages of progress. Here also only tangible property is considered. This can hardly be called a rough approximation to real values. The operations of this scheme cause the wild fluctuations exhibited in the brief table below:

ASSESSMENT OF STREET CARS.[32]

County.	Cost of plant.	Assessed value.	Per cent of cost.
Atchison	$425,000	$25,400	5.9
Bourbon	124,000	9,120	7.3
Cowley	49,241	200	.4
Cowley	25,000	220	.8
Crawford	134,050	6,000	4.4
Leavenworth	85,438	35,150	41.1
	$842,729	$76,090	9.

Interurban and intercounty car lines are rapidly multiplying and promise to produce even wider disparities in assessment than the above, unless state assessment is provided.

Insurance companies constitute a form of corporation that the state also finds it difficult to tax wisely. Their tangible property—what little they may have—is assessed and taxed through the local agencies. The state insurance department exacts fees of different kinds, amounting practically to a tax. Every fire insurance company doing business in a city where there is a fire department worth $1,000 or more, must pay to the superintendent of insurance $2 on every $100 received from premiums on fire and lightning policies within that city. This money then goes into the funds of the Firemen's Relief Association of the various cities, now 112 in number, meeting the requirements. In 1897, $16,239.90 was received from this source; in 1900, $20,640.26; in 1901, $22,561.95.

---

[31] *Genl. Stat.*, 1901, ch. 107, art. 5.
[32] 13 *Bureau of Labor*, 1897, p. 118-20.

Still further exactions are made of foreign insurance companies doing business in the state. For several years they paid annually to the insurance department 2 per cent. on all premiums received. In 1898 this was increased to a payment of 4 per cent. on all premiums received during the year.

The insurance department costs the state from $6,000 to $9,000 a year, but returns in the way of taxes and fees some $130,000.[33]

In June, 1902, 211 insurance companies were doing business in the state.

The foregoing account of assessment, supplemented as it is with numerous concrete and authentic examples, is deemed sufficient to show the gross excess of inequalities prevailing under present methods. These are necessary evils while the present "system" remains in force. To level off the worst of these inequalities there is employed the machinery of state and county boards of "equalization." The three commissioners in each county sit as a board of equalization when the assessment returns are all in the hands of the county clerk, and it is their duty to inspect the valuations returned for all the property in the county, to listen to all complaints, and to equalize the assessments made by the several assessors by raising or lowering the values as they see fit. The abstract of this assessment roll as thus "equalized" goes before the state board of equalization (secretary of state, auditor,

---

[33] Receipts of Insurance Department:

	1900	1901
For agents' licenses	$19,401 00	$17,951 75
For charter fees	1,190 00	830 00
For annual statements	7,275 00	7,780 00
For State school fund	6,300 00	6,650 00
For taxes	75,698 96	82,025 44
For examinations	....	2,013 46
For firemen's relief fund	20,640 26	22,561 95
For miscellaneous fees	97 70	97 36
	$130,602 92	$139,909 96

Expenditures of Insurance Department:

	1900	1901
Maintenance of department	$6,734 07	$9,087 70
Firemen's relief fund	20,640 26	22,561 95
	$27,374 33	$31,649 66

and treasurer). This board tries to strike a rough justice among the counties by raising the assessment of one county 10 per cent., lowering another 5 per cent., and so on, but not reducing the aggregate assessment. (However, it is sometimes necessary to lower the aggregate assessment, the statute to the contrary notwithstanding.) County attorneys appear before the board and ask for reductions, when they fear their county is likely to pay more state tax than its share.

But the task before these boards is too great for them or any similar board to perform. Such chaotic assessments cannot be equalized, and the most that is accomplished is merely to mitigate the evils and thus perpetuate a bad system. Since no assessment is either high or low, except in comparison with some other assessment, and no man knows his neighbor's assessment, it follows that few men appear before the county boards of equalization and ask for a change in their valuation. The few men who do appear are not as a rule men with the small holdings and whose assessments are the highest.

When this so-called equalization is completed, the next steps are the levy and collection of taxes. The county commissioners levy and apportion the county taxes among the townships. The township trustee levies the township tax. In school districts the school tax is levied or voted at the annual school meeting, after the fashion of the early New England town meetings. But in cities of the first and second class, the school district is coterminous with the city, and here a board of education makes the levy. The city tax, like all its other financial matters, is in the hands of the city council.

But the great anomaly appears in the levy of the state tax. The state legislature determines not only the amount to be raised, *but also the rate.* That is, in substance they say at their biennial session, we will raise $2,000,000 a year for the next two years, and the rate shall be 5 mills on the dollar. This levy is always made in the early spring, several months before that year's assessment returns are in, to which this rate shall apply. Hence the levy must be based on the assessment returns of the preceding year. This imposes the preposterous duty on the state board of equalization of patching up the assessment returns to fit the arbitrary and senseless rate fixed by the legislature. If the returns happen to be about the same as the year before, no change in their aggregate is needed. But great fluctuations are likely to occur, and do frequently occur. Thus from 1898 to 1900 there was an increase in assessed valuations of $17,000,000. At the rate of the state levy, this would have raised a surplus revenue of $93,000. From 1883 to 1884 the increase was $33,800,000. From 1887 to 1888 the increase was $42,300,000. The 1900 assessment returns showed an increase over the preceding year of $13,500,000. On this basis, the levy by the legislature would have returned $80,000 of surplus revenue. The state board could not change the rate to fit the needs, so lowered the assessment returns by $11,675,044. So the law declaring such aggregate shall not be lowered fails to operate. For the support of the State University, the legislature does appropriate a stated amount, and the rate necessary to produce this amount is adjusted by the state board. Why this rational plan is not applied to all other appropriations is difficult to comprehend. That it is legal has already been decided by the supreme court of the state, where the opinion was rendered that "The legislature may levy taxes by requiring a gross sum to be collected from the taxable property of the state as well as by fixing a rate per cent.[34]

The chief evils of this system are not its awkwardness and inconvenience. The worst feature in this levying of a certain *rate* of taxation by the legislature rather than appropriating a definite sum, is the fact that should the local divisions ever desire to obey the law and raise their assessment of property to the "actual value in money," then the general state revenue would swell to four or five times its normal size. Thus the evil of underassessment is intrenched and perpetuated.

Collection of taxes is effected through the county treasurers, whether the taxes are state or local. The treasurers receive the completed tax roll from the county clerks. The auditor of state notifies the county what its portion of state tax is, the apportionment being made, of course, on the basis of the "equalized" returns from the state board of equalization. The county must then furnish this sum, or be held liable for delinquent taxes.

---

[34] 56 *Kans.*, 81.

It is then a matter of indifferece to the county whether it uses its own equalized assessment as basis of levy and collection, or takes the equalized returns from the state board, for the state board has only modified it as lump sum. For the county fol. lows the rational method and djusts the levy to fit the appro. priation, the fresh assessment rurns being the basis of the levy. Those industries assessed by th state board, such as railroads, telegraph, etc., pay their taxes ocally, according to the values assigned to each county, townsip, school district and city. For since there is no separation of te sources of revenue, the state, like the school district, has its revnue collected and remitted by the county treasurer.[23]

Taxes are due and payable i the county treasurers on and after November 1. Half may b paid by December 20, and half six months later. If the secon half is paid by December 20, a 5 per cent. rebate on it is graned. If either half remains un. paid when due, a 5 per cent. cnalty is added. Ample pro. visions are made for the sale of oth personal and real property for unpaid taxes. On the wholethe system of collection is on a fairly sound business basis.

Some observations are timely i closing this discussion of taxa. tion. We have seen that, lackin any central supervision, each local assessor is a law unto himsel. In the words of that worthy Kansan, J. G. Haskell,[24] "every assessor does that which is right in his own eyes and there is n sufficient supervising author. ity. * * * Legislation is inadequat. The clash of diverse inter-

---

[23] The total taxes paid by railroads amount to about $2,000,000 a year. From auditor's reports it appears that the taxes have been as follows:

1892	$1,739,253
1893	2,065,419
1895	2,071,724
1897	2,119,875
1899	2,203,978
1901	1,968,965

This is about one-sixth of all taxes paid d the state. The total taxes paid by railroads up to 1901, are approximately $41,790,000. The total subsidies received by the roads for same time, are $4,716,356.

[24] Captain Haskel of Lawrence, Kansas, e over forty years a taxpayer of the state, and best known as the architect of he state capitol, came with the New England migration to aid the free-state cause. As a trained scholar and substantial citizen, he is peculiarly well qualind to speak. The quotation above is from a private letter of December 13, 190.

ests, coupled with the effort) secure equality under unequal
conditions ("equal treatmet of unequals"') militates against
good legislation. • • • There defective enforcement of the law.
The tax laws must bristle wh clear. stringent and arbitrary
provisions. All enforcing olers should be removed from local
politics."

Full publicity of assessmets is one reform demanded by all
persons familiar with the ils of the present system. Each
taxpayer should know his on and his neighbor's assessment.
A permanent state tax boar r commission is also imperatively
demanded. and under this her county boards. or county assessors with deputies. Separtion of the sources of state and
local revenue would then take the machinery of the state
board of equalization whol unnecessary. These reforms are
suggested here, not becaus hey are remedies for all the ills
of the present system. but because they are steps in a forward
direction. already taken by progressive states such as New York.
Pennsylvania. and Wisconn: and are compatible with the
Kansas constitution. Nothig has been gained thus far. or is
likely to be gained of permnent good. through mere legislative
committees.

Fiscal Affairs.—Moneys i the state treasury are credited to
certain funds which are eil. r permanent or annual; the most
important annual fund bein the general revenue fund. Salaries
of state officers. and experes for the general conduct of the
state government are all pai from this fund. The largest fund
is. of course. the permanen school fund. This is invested first
in Kansas state bonds. and ien in such local bonds as are available. The present state dot (January. 1904) of $632,000 is
all held in the permanent scool funds.—$9.000 in the University
fund, and $623,00 in the ommon school fund. Transfers of
money from one fund to aother are common. when the fund
is not a permanent one. his happens sometimes to the sinking fund— as in 1902. wha it was transferred, *in toto,* to the
general revenue fund.

Interest on the state bods was commonly made payable at
some selected bank in NewYork City. known as the state fiscal
agency. Here all couponswere clipped and bonds paid when

It is then a matter of indifference to the county whether it uses its own equalized assessment as a basis of levy and collection, or takes the equalized returns from the state board, for the state board has only modified it as a lump sum. For the county follows the rational method and adjusts the levy to fit the appropriation, the fresh assessment returns being the basis of the levy. Those industries assessed by the state board, such as railroads, telegraph, etc., pay their taxes locally, according to the values assigned to each county, township, school district and city. For since there is no separation of the sources of revenue, the state, like the school district, has its revenue collected and remitted by the county treasurer.[35]

Taxes are due and payable to the county treasurers on and after November 1. Half may be paid by December 20, and half six months later. If the second half is paid by December 20, a 5 per cent. rebate on it is granted. If either half remains unpaid when due, a 5 per cent. penalty is added. Ample provisions are made for the sale of both personal and real property for unpaid taxes. On the whole, the system of collection is on a fairly sound business basis.

Some observations are timely in closing this discussion of taxation. We have seen that, lacking any central supervision, each local assessor is a law unto himself. In the words of that worthy Kansan, J. G. Haskell,[36] "every assessor does that which is right in his own eyes and there is no sufficient supervising authority. * * * Legislation is inadequate. The clash of diverse inter-

---

[35] The total taxes paid by railroads amount to about $2,000,000 a year. From auditor's reports it appears that these taxes have been as follows:

1892	$1,739,353
1893	2,065,419
1895	2,071,724
1897	2,119,875
1899	2,203,978
1901	1,968,965

This is about one-sixth of all taxes paid in the state. The total taxes paid by railroads up to 1901, are approximately, $41,790,000. The total subsidies received by the roads for same time, are $43,718,356.

[36] Captain Haskel of Lawrence, Kansas, for over forty years a taxpayer of the state, and best known as the architect of the state capitol, came with the New England migration to aid the free-state cause. As a trained scholar and substantial citizen, he is peculiarly well qualified to speak. The quotation above is from a private letter of December 18, 1903.

ests, coupled with the effort to secure equality under unequal conditions ("equal treatment of unequals") militates against good legislation. * * * There is defective enforcement of the law. The tax laws must bristle with clear, stringent and arbitrary provisions. All enforcing officers should be removed from local politics.'

Full publicity of assessments is one reform demanded by all persons familiar with the evils of the present system. Each taxpayer should know his own and his neighbor's assessment. A permanent state tax board or commission is also imperatively demanded, and under this either county boards, or county assessors with deputies. Separation of the sources of state and local revenue would then make the machinery of the state board of equalization wholly unnecessary. These reforms are suggested here, not because they are remedies for all the ills of the present system, but because they are steps in a forward direction, already taken by progressive states such as New York, Pennsylvania, and Wisconsin; and are compatible with the Kansas constitution. Nothing has been gained thus far, or is likely to be gained of permanent good, through mere legislative committees.

Fiscal Affairs.—Moneys in the state treasury are credited to certain funds which are either permanent or annual; the most important annual fund being the general revenue fund. Salaries of state officers, and expenses for the general conduct of the state government are all paid from this fund. The largest fund is, of course, the permanent school fund. This is invested first in Kansas state bonds, and then in such local bonds as are available. The present state debt (January, 1904) of $632,000 is all held in the permanent school funds,—$9.000 in the University fund, and $623,00 in the common school fund. Transfers of money from one fund to another are common, when the fund is not a permanent one. This happens sometimes to the sinking fund— as in 1902, when it was transferred, *in toto,* to the general revenue fund.

Interest on the state bonds was commonly made payable at some selected bank in New York City, known as the state fiscal agency. Here all coupons were clipped and bonds paid when due, the state paying one-fourth of one per cent. commission for the service. Latterly when the state bought up some of its own bonds before due, and had to forward them to New York to have the coupons clipped, the practice 'was inaugurated of making both bonds and interest payable at home. This is now the custom with all small bond issues that can be floated in the home market.

The budget, or estimate of expenditures for the next two years, is prepared by the auditor in time to be presented with the governor's message to each newly-convened legislature. All moneys must be voted every two years, according to the constitution. This of course holds the state institutions to a stricter accountability. This is doubtless salutary in the long run, but not infrequently the State University has been made to suffer from spasms of economy which sometimes overtake the legislature. The fiscal year closed November 30, as long as the sessions of the legislature were annual; but beginning with the biennial session in 1877, the close of the fiscal year has been June 30. Thus the legislature of 1901 makes appropriations covering the period which ends June 30, 1903. In January, 1903, the legislature convenes and reappropriates a part of this money for legislative expenses. Thus the incoming legislature commences to spend money at once, but the revenue which it provides does not begin to come in till about one year later.

The passage of the budget to a vote is in most points similar to the course pursued by Congress with its committee system. The part of the governor's mesasge on finance is referred by each house to its ways and means committee. This is a large, standing committee, usually having nine members in the Senate and seventeen in the House. These two form a joint ways and means committee to consider all general appropriation bills. These bills may originate in either house. Bills recommended by the joint ways and means committee are then discussed by the houses in the committee of the whole. In the rush towards the end of the session a "revision committee" may revise the list of bills and strike off a few, thus precluding their coming to a vote. This, of course, is not likely to happen to any important revenue measure.

The law has provided all the treasury machinery deemed necessary for the custody of the state funds. The deposit system is not yet adopted, although the need of it is well established by the experiences of the past. All moneys are to be kept in the treasury, except the amount with the New York fiscal agency necessary to meet maturing interest and bonds. This agency pays 2 per cent. interest on average daily balances. This would seem to suggest that a few hundred thousand of other state funds might be wisely deposited in good banks, thus providing the state an interest-income of a few thousand a year, and affording circulation to otherwise idle capital. To safeguard the treasury, the law calls for its monthly examination by the governor, secretary, and auditor, and also further provides for inspection by a legislative committee and an expert accountant whenever necessary. It is physically impossible, however, for the governor, secretary, and auditor to make an adequate inspection as often as the law demands, and perform the other duties of their offices. Hence this law is not obeyed.

The treasurer is bound by a solemn oath and by a bond of $1,000,000. The auditor also takes a formal oath, and gives a bond for $10,000. The auditor and treasurer are to serve as checks and balances against each other. The auditor must keep account of all appropriations, audit all accounts of moneys paid out of the treasury; and issue his warrant on the treasurer for amounts due by law. The treasurer is custodian of all state funds, and through his office all income must pass and all expenditures be made.

A closing word must be said on the subject of banking. Now that the system has recovered from the financial panic of '93 and '94, and the "house-cleaning process" of the state bank commissioner has been completed, the banks have entered upon a period of sound expansion. The use of bank checks and bank credits is rapidly spreading in the transaction of business throughout the entire state. Thus in the period of 1899 and 1900, while deposits increased over $9,000,000, the actual cash held by the banks increased only $178,100. This element of elasticity in the state's monetary mediums, under the wise surveillance of the state bank commissioner, is a mark of progress

[141]

in the economic life of the state. The character of the bank deposits in the years 1900 and 1902 proves very interesting as shown in the table below:[37]

KANSAS BANK DEPOSITORS CLASSIFIED.

	1900.	Per cent.	1902.	Per cent.
Total number of depositors......	111,132	100	139,167	100
Male.	89,533	80.5	113,061	81.2
Female	16,938	15.2	21,354	15.3
Farmers and stockmen	60,992	55.	76,938	55.2
Merchants..........................	8,909	8.	11,695	8.
Public accounts........	2,345	2.1	3,526	2.5
Accounts of corporations	1,516	1.3	1,455	1.
Farmers' and stockmen's deposits	$517,839,318	56.5	$27,240,317	68.0
Public accounts...................	2.533,005	8.0	3,204,653	8.0
Corporations.,..............	2,058,067	6.5	2,002,964	5.0

Conclusion.—It is not within the province of this history to devise remedies for such evils as exist in the present financial system of Kansas, but rather to report facts as they are, whatever they may be. It is hoped that both the good and the bad features of this system have been impartially and accurately set forth. Since reform cannot come suddenly, but must follow the slow course of an evolutionary growth, it is the sincere hope of the writer that this reform may take the direction of a gradual displacement of the general property tax. Then, with a proper segregation of the sources of revenue, there may be introduced a revenue system calculated to distribute its burdens justly and wisely, from both the fiscal and social standpoints.

Not till some constitutional limitations are removed. however, can the tax power be employed for important social purposes in addition to its fiscal uses. Certain provisions regarding an imaginary "equality" are a barrier to this. In the matter of expenditure the state is freer from constitutional limitations. Hence there is a constantly expanding outlay as the state undertakes to meet growing wants and supply new needs. This taking on of new functions, however, has not only been necessary, but wise, and its growth in the future will likely remain un-

[37] 5 and 6 *Bien. Reports, Kansas Bank Com.*

checked.   For, as our great economists have shown, taxation increases with freedom.[38]

In spite of the rigid system of financial administration and the shortcomings of the systems of outlay and income, the outlook is not bad.   Light is breaking, as is evidenced by the increasing attention directed to this subject by each succeeding legislature of recent years, and especially by the legislature of 1901 in its creation of a temporary tax commission of able men.

[38] Ely, *Outlines of Economics,* p. 356.   Dr. Ely here shows that small expenditures mean small results ; despotic Russia spends 13 cents per capita for schools ; but Zurich, Switzerland, $1.25.

CHAPTER IX

FINANCIAL HISTORY OF TOPEKA, KANSAS

As late as the beginning of the Civil War, Topeka was little more than a straggling group of log huts on the banks of the Kansas or Kaw river. The city dates its founding back to the year 1854, when seven persons—the front edge, as it were, of the wave of Kansas Territory migration—made this their permanent stopping place. Within three years the little group had increased to five hundred souls, and Topeka became an incorporated village. The outbreak of the war caused a heavy shrinkage in population, for nearly every able-bodied man within the age-limits enlisted as a soldier.

Not till 1861 did Topeka succeed in making good her metropolitan claims over her neighbors. This year, with a population of some six hundred souls, the little city was made the capital of the state. From this time population rapidly increased till the "hard times" of the early seventies set in. Then followed another period of rapid expansion, till the reaction of the nineties caused a temporary setback. This was a period of decline for many cites of the Middle West, a great many of them showing an actual falling-off in population. Topeka, however, managed to hold its own. Gains were made at each census from 1860 on, but very fluctuating gains, to be sure. These fluctuations run as follows: from 1860 to 1865 the gain was 70 per cent.; from 1865 to 1870, 330 per cent.; from 1870 to 1875, 25 per cent.; from 1875 to 1880, 115 per cent.; from 1880 to 1885, 74 per cent.; from 1885 to 1890, 31 per cent.; from 1890 to 1900, 8 per cent. These variations in the figures are due to various "boom" periods, to a heavy immigration of colored people from the South during the seventies, and to general conditions affecting the prosperity of the West. The census of 1860 showed a population of 759; the 1900 census, 33,608. The great Kaw river floods of 1903 and 1904 caused a heavy exodus which will doubtless affect the next census returns.

When Topeka reached a population of 15,000 (in 1880), it became, under the general laws of the state, a city of the first class. The same laws or "charter" apply to all cities of this class in the state.

The charter of Topeka is very liberal in its grant of powers. In things financial, almost complete autonomy is enjoyed. However, in one important matter—the regulation of the liquor traffic—the city occupies a peculiar and anomalous position. The city cannot license and supervise this business, because the state constitution peremptorily prohibits all manufacture and sale of intoxicants within the state. And, on the other hand, the federal government issues permits to sell intoxicants, regardless of all city or state regulations. Hence the city has a vigorous traffic, carried on by drug stores with federal permits, which is wholly unamenable to municipal or state rules. The city must look on, supinely, then, while the liquor traffic flourishes in her midst, bringing her not only no revenue, but actually increasing her police-court expenditures. Some other cities of the state do have open saloons, contrary to law, and "fine" them stated sums once a month instead of licensing them for the same amount. Topeka seems to demonstrate, however, that so far as her fiscal life is concerned, she has no need whatever of saloons, and, indeed, prospers best without them. Common observation of the cities of the state verifies this claim.

A few specific provisons of the city's charter may well claim our attention at this point. The duties of the mayor are clearly set forth in these words: "He shall from time to time communicate to the council, in writing, such information and recommend such measures as in his opinion may tend to the improvement of the finances of the city, the police, health, security, ornament, comfort and general prosperity of the city."[1] As a matter of fact, the mayor does not "communicate in writing" to the council, so this provision remains up to the present a dead letter. But as to the broad functions of the city-corporation, we see them outlined in the words, "improvement of the finances of the city, the police, health, security, ornament, comfort and

---

[1] *Revised Ordinances of 1888*, Art. IV, sec. 44.

general prosperity of the city.'' The city is thus like a state within a state, an *imperium in imperio*. In carrying out these various functions, in providing for its own health and security, its own comfort and ornamentation, the city must receive and disburse considerable revenue.

Topeka's charter provides that the public utilities—water, light and street railways—may, at the option of the city, be owned by the city.[2] (1) As to water. The city may grant a thirty-year franchise, and as a consideration therefor, must require ten per cent. of net earnings of the company, over and above eight per cent. on the investment, after deducting the reasonable cost of maintenance, operation and taxes. The city may acquire the plant after ten years from the time of granting the franchise. The price shall be set by three commissioners (one selected by the city, one by the company, and one an engineer, by the judge of the court). A popular vote shall then decide whether to take the property at that price, and if the decision is an affirmative one, the city may issue thirty-year bonds at six per cent. or less. (2) As to light, heat, power, and street railways. The charter provides here that the city may grant a thirty-year franchise and may extend the same another thirty years. The consideration shall be ten per cent. of the net earnings, over and above ten per cent. earnings on the investment. The city may acquire the plant at expiration of franchise.

We see therefore, in the foregoing, what the city *may* do under its charter. What is actually done in the matter of these public utilities we shall discuss in detail under appropriate paragraphs below. But it should be distinctly stated here that the street car, gas and water companies pay the city nothing for their franchises. There are other activities of a quasi-public and a private nature, into which the city must enter in the performance of its diversified functions. We shall examine, therefore, all expenditures of the city in the living of its full life, in the fulfilment of its every function of whatever nature. The significant facts in the growth of city expenditures will be duly pointed out. This will lead naturally to a consideration of the city's income,

---

[2] *Laws of Kansas*, 1903, ch. 122.

its sources, methods of collection, etc. The city will be seen here in various roles, from that of a simple owner of income-bearing property, to that of a sovereign imposing taxes upon subjects. This will be followed with a discussion of the municipal debt, fiscal machinery and city accounting. This last offers a rich field for criticism, for as a press writer has so ably said:[3] "City finance is such a confusing and altogether hopeless tangle of discordant bookkeeping, that the city clerks' reports on current receipts and expenses are rather more likely to be misleading than to give to the average citizen a clear idea of the condition of affairs. The calendar year overlaps the fiscal year, and the tax receipts overlap both."

EXPENDITURES

The city's life and functions are well exhibited by its expenditures from year to year. The following table is accordingly given showing fifteen important objects of outlay during six years. It is unfortunately impossible to go farther back than 1892 in any accounts, since the records prior to this date are lost or destroyed. From 1892 to 1897 faulty bookkeeping vitiates the records to such an extent that they cannot be used for comparisons or conveniently tabulated. Hence the table below exhibits expenditures from 1897 to 1902, inclusive:

EXPENDITURES, 1897–1902

Object	1897	1898	1899	1900	1901	1902
Education	$90,514	$100,629	$150,093	$155,198	$192,028	$144,205
Fire	26,718	27,907	26,177	28,230	29,827	28,809
Water............	36,975	....	29,000	14,500	14,877	....
Police............	22,145	23,336	20,297	20,939	23,636	26,573
Light	20,063	13,924	11,197	18,751	19,599	14,187
Health	5,098	4,431	4,232	9,013	9,094	11,993
Streets...........	42,186	198,586	87,703	159,130	289,342	184,887
Parks	445	119	555	4,597	4,664	11,647
Buildings and improvements	12,911	4,612	2,313	43,158	66,874	722
Admin. salaries...	11,784	12,674	10,043	15,446	21,670	21,883
Judgments........	35,666	14,787	6,109	4,363	3,158	2,072
Elections	2,650	2,805	3,597	3,271	3,317	3,500
Printing	858	844	1,084	1,796	1,353	2,830
Library	6,942	5,020	3,827	5,922	3,770	6,044
Subsidies	....	....	....	75	60,248	....
Totals.......	$314,955	$409,674	$356,227	$484,389	$743,457	$449,349

[3] *Topeka State Journal.* Sept. 6, 1904. p. 10.

This table represents but fifteen of the important functions of the city, chosen because satisfactory statistics were available. But, choosing 1897 as a typical year, we find that the city expended for all purposes the following amounts:

Education	$90,514
Fire	26,718
Water	36,975
Police	22,145
Light	20,063
Health	5,098
Streets	42,186
Parks	445
Buildings and improvements	12,911
Administrative salaries	11,784
Interest on debt	16,805
Judgments	35,666
Miscellaneous	2,161
Elections	2,560
Printing	858
Library	6,942
Total	$333,831

Charity.—Charity, it will be noticed, does not appear in the list above. This is for the reason that the city poor are considered county poor, and hence obtain relief through the county officials, at county expense. There is a regular county one-mill tax-levy for the poor. This unquestionably places some undue burdens on the rural districts of the county, but custom has adjusted the yoke to their necks. There seems to be little thought of change.

Attention must now be directed in some detail to the separate functions of the city, that a clearer understanding of them be obtained. We find them today evolutionary growths, and in process of further evolution.

Education.—The city maintains an efficient graded school system, including a city high school and a manual training high school. The high schools are used in common by white and colored children, as are many of the ward schools. In certain parts of the city, however, where the colored population predominates, separate schools of equal rank are provided for the colored children. This is in accordance with the city charter.

Expenditure for schools is divided into three heads; namely, (1) general fund, or maintenance, (2) interest and sinking fund, to meet maturing bonds, and (3) building or construction account. In 1903, when the assessed valuation of the city was $11,000,000, the levy for these different purposes was as follows:

General fund (maintenance).................12 mills,	or	$132,000
Interest and sinking fund.....................1 mill,	or	11,000
Building ....3 mills,	or	33,000
Total ....16 mills,	or	$176,000

The school levy shows a decided tendency to increase with the increase in population. For example, this has been the course since 1892:

Year	Levy in mills
1892	9.8
1893	9.8
1894	10.0
1895	10.0
1896	10.0
1897	10.0
1898	11.0
1899	16.0
1900	16.0
1901	15.5
1903	16.0

This is not due, however, to a per capita increase in outlay for schools, as the bald statistics would seem to prove, but is due rather to the growing evil of under-assessment.

The different sources of revenue for city schools may be seen at once by a glance at the table below:

TOTAL INCOME FOR SCHOOLS FOR THE YEAR ENDING JUNE, 1904

Balance from last year............................	$2,152 39
Taxes	191,610 97
From school fund.................................	11,417 95
Interest (bank deposits)..........................	364 02
Tuition	2,024 50
Sale of material..................................	148 93
Rents	30 00
Miscellaneous	188 85
Sale of bonds....................................	122,000 00
Total	$329,937 61

Fire.—Like other cities, Topeka first depended upon a volunteer fire department. In 1870 the city purchased a Sibley steam fire engine, and a volunteer fire company was organized. Improvements were gradually introduced during the next few years, and a small compensation was allowed the members of the company. "The chief, G. O. Wilmarth, laid the foundation of the present full-paid system. in 1876, by selecting sixteen of the best and most efficient men from the volunteer service as it then existed. This force was then placed under a thorough drill, and paid a fair compensation for their services to the city."[4]

Prior to public water (1882) the company depended upon wells and cisterns. The first substantial building for the department, a stone structure, was erected in 1873. The next year a building was erected for the chemical engine.

In 1882 the Gamewell Fire Alarm Telegraph system was introduced at a cost of $3,225. At the present time (1904) it comprises about 33 miles of telegraph wires, 50 fire alarm signal boxes, one 4-circuit electric repeater in the fire marshal's office, and other apparatus necessary to complete its efficiency.

The department now is composed of thirty well-drilled officers and men permanently employed. There are four fire stations, equipped throughout with good modern apparatus. The water service for fire protection is the "direct pressure" system, comprising 322 fire hydrants, with about 45 miles of water mains, the diameter of the mains running from 4 inches to 18 inches. The yearly losses by fire have been kept at a very low figure,— $36,312 in 1901, $19,379 in 1902.

The expenditures for this department have showed a tendency to remain almost stationary, despite the growth of the city. The following table shows the amounts expended for the maintenance of this department since 1892:

1892	$27,634
1893	27,473
1895	27,124
1897	26,718
1898	27,907
1899	26,177
1900	28,230
1901	29,827
1902	28,809

[4] Giles, *Thirty Years of Topeka*, p. 398.

According to the value of the service rendered, this is undoubtedly one of the cheapest departments of city government.

Water.—We have already noted the provisions in the charter concerning water. In 1881 a proposal was made to construct a municipal plant at a cost of $281,000, but the proposal was defeated. A franchise was then given (without compensation) for twenty years to a private company. This company received the usual rights and privileges to use city streets, alleys, etc., for water pipes, with the condition that they repair the street torn up in laying or repairing pipes. Other conditions met by the company were: (1) the capacity of the plant should be 3,000,000 gallons, fire pressure, in 24 hours; (2) there should be 15 miles at least of mains and distributing pipes, 4 to 16 inches in diameter; (3) the city council should designate route of pipes; (4) the city obligated itself, at the end of 20 years to extend the franchise for 20 years, or to acquire the plant on "paying therefor the fair and equitable value thereof;" (5) the company should give a clear title; (6) the city rented for 20 years 150 hydrants at $7,000 a year; additional hydrants should be furnished, if desired, at $50 a year; each future extension of pipe should furnish the city 10 hydrants per mile, for $500 a year; when number of hydrants should reach 300, city might demand all its new ones, when needed, free of rental; (7) the city should have free water for flushing streets, fire department, city buildings, public schools, fountains, etc.; (8) lastly, the amount and quality of water and rates therefor should be regulated by city ordinance.

These conditions being duly accepted by the Topeka Water Supply Company, a private corporation, a Holly water system was put into operation in 1882.

There has been more or less dissatisfaction with the franchise. In 1897 the city paid to the water company hydrant rental for two and a half years, the sum of $36,975, on the order of the United States District Court. The voters of the city have not yet been ready to pay the price for the plant and place it under municipal ownership. Hence the system remains one of mere city regulation of private property.

Light.—Topeka, in common with many other cities, was con-

.vinced of the value of the tower-system of street lighting, when
this system first came into vogue. Accordingly, in the spring
of 1882, the city council entered into a contract to have seven
towers, 150 feet high, erected in different parts of the city, for
the sum of $6,000. These were to display electric lights of the
Brush patent; other parties were under contract to furnish
electricity. The first tower finished proved a dangerous thing to
keep in order, and a sickening disappointment as to its lighting
powers. The other towers were never finished, the city com-
promising by paying $2,700. The one tower was soon put out
of use, and the whole scheme proved a costly fiasco.

The present plant is a municipal plant, owned and operated
by the city. It was built in 1888, at a cost of $55,448.[5] Its
capacity was 184 arc lights for street lighting only (incandescent
lights are furnished by a private company). The present plant
represents an outlay for construction of $85,000, and the number
of arc lamps is now 342. According to municipal bookkeeping
the cash cost of operating the plant for the year ending December 31, 1902, a typical year, was $12,357.90. The total cost of
"operating, maintenance, interest and depreciation" was
$18,308. The cash cost per lamp for the year was thus $36.13;
the total cost per arc lamp per year, $53.53. The plant was run
on a moonlight schedule, 2,296 hours. This is the printed statement of the department. It has been challenged, however. A
prominent financier, thoroughly familiar with the subject says;
"In general, as to the accounting in the city lighting plant, I
have known for years that it was very unsatisfactory, that they
included in their statements only the actual cash expenditures
directly chargeable against the plant, and that even then, certain expenses which ought properly to be charged to the plant,
got into the other accounts. No provision was ever made for
depreciation, and the plant has been wearing out and they have
now to face the problem of a very serious expenditure in order
to maintain the present lights, or to give the additional service
which the people demand. The fact is, that the entire business
has been handled with the apparent desire to make the cost of

---

[5] Statement (Leaflet) of City El. Light. Dept., H. K. Goodrich, Supt., Topeka,
1903.

operation just as low as possible because each administration has taken a certain degree of credit for the results, and has pointed with pride to the low cost of lighting as compared with lighting offers which have been made by the local commercial plant.''

Police.—The police function is a fundamental one. We see it exercised from the days of the ''marshall'' of the village, on a small stipendium, to the present city force of full paid, uniformed, police officers. It was in the year 1872 that a city prison and police station was erected. The growth of the outlay for the maintenance of this department, both by absolute and per capita amounts, is shown in the table below:

EXPENDITURES FOR POLICE DEPARTMENT MAINTENANCE, 1892–1902.

Year.	Amount.	Per capita amount.
1892	$19,578	.62
1893	18,180	.57
1894	18,329	.57
1895	23,454	.72
1896	21,619	.66
1897	22,145	.67
1898	23,336	.70
1899	20,927	.61
1900	20,939	.62
1901	23,636	.70
1902	26,573	.78

The running expenses of this department are about five times the amount taken in by the city in fines and penalties.

Health.—The board of health of the city consists of three men, the secretary of the board being the city physician. He devotes but part of his time to this office, and receives a compensation of $600 a year. This department enforces a quarantine in all cases of contagious diseases, maintains a free dispensary, looks after the burying of dead animals, cremation of garbage, etc. Expenses fluctuate greatly from year to year, depending wholly upon unforeseen causes. Thus during the fiscal year 1900, the city was put to an outlay of $5,000 on account of an epidemic known as the Cuban Chickenpox. The average outlay now varies from $10,000 to $12,000 a year. The growth of the outlay shows a tendency to keep pace with the growth of the city.

[153]

Library.—The beginning of the present city library was a public reading room started by a few women in 1870. From this grew a free public library. The city in 1877 granted a subsidy of $100 a month, and later increased the amount. The state then gave the right of "perpetual occupancy" of part of the capitol grounds (200 feet by 200 feet), and a $44,000 library building was erected here in 1880. The cost of the building was defrayed by private donations of local citizens.

The city now makes appropriations for the maintenance of the library, as given in the table below:

LIBRARY OUTLAY

1892	$4,085
1893	6,153
1894	2,968
1895	5,141
1896	3,624
1897	6,942
1898	5,020
1899	3,827
1900	5,922
1901	3,770
1902	6,044

A half-mill tax-levy is now customary for this purpose.

Streets.—The first public improvement on record was the improvement of streets. At a meeting of the council, March 24, 1858, the marshall was authorized to grade the "street between the end of the bridge and First Avenue," at an expenditure not exceeding $150.[6]

Construction and maintenance of streets represent, next to education, the highest item of expense in the city's budget. This is due largely to the unusual width of the streets and to the large amount of paving. Beginning to pave in 1887, during the next sixteen years the city expended for paving (including grading, curbing, etc.) the sum of $1,543,015, or practically, $100,000 a year. The first pavement laid was Lake Trinidad asphalt, an expensive material. Most of the asphalt streets now are in a deplorable condition, caused to some extent by the use of inferior materials in construction, and also to some extent

---

[6] Giles, p. 126 ff.

by neglect in cleaning and carelessness in repairing. In 1897 the city made a contract for the repairing and keeping in repair of the asphalt pavement for a term of five years at $8,000 a year.[7] At the expiration of this contract in 1902, another contract was entered into for five years, a paving company agreeing to keep the asphalt streets in repair at $1.58 per square yard. This is costing the city three or four thousand dollars a year, and considering the present condition of the pavement, is looked upon as a useless expenditure of money. A few asphalt streets will likely be resurfaced and preserved, while others, where traffic is heavy, will likely be superseded by other kinds of paving material.

The first brick pavement was laid in 1890 at a cost of $1.78 per square yard. Two courses of brick were laid on sand with a sand filler. The method proved satisfactory, cost little for repairs, and is still in use. The cost now, however, runs from $1.12½ to $1.25 for the same grade of work.

Where traffic is very heavy, the city paved with Colorado sandstone (1887–1889). In March, 1890, contrary to the advice of the city engineer, the city let the contract for paving a heavy business street (Sixth Avenue East) with native limestone. Within a few years this pavement was almost entirely disintegrated.

A few streets were paved during 1887–1888 with cedar blocks, but this too, is practically worn out.

Topeka on January 1, 1903, had 669,518 square yards or 32.23 miles of pavement, divided as to material as follows:

```
Brick  ..........................371,276 sq. yds., or 19.58 miles
Asphalt  ........................193,810 sq. yds., or  7.1  miles
Red Cedar blocks ................ 34,445 sq. yds., or  1.45 miles
Colorado sandstone .............. 51,642 sq. yds., or  2.4  miles
Native limestone ................ 10,578 sq. yds., or  1.1  miles
Macadam  ........................  7,767 sq. yds., or  0.6  miles
```

The outlay for streets is met by issuing internal improvement bonds (street paving bonds, alley paving bonds, sewer and drain bonds). The city pays only for those improvements made at crossings. The bulk of the expense falls, therefore, on

---

[7] City Ordinance. No. 1881. Approved Aug. 31. 1896.

abutting property, under a special assessment on the "benefit district," as described under special assessment below.

Parks.—Topeka spends but little for parks, and has but little to show for it. Not till 1900, when the population numbered 33,608, was a park commission created. Three or four thousand dollars a year since that time has been appropriated by the city for the few small parks within the city limits. These aggregate but 22.91 acres, the largest containing but 12 acres. The city also owns 80 acres one mile and a half west of the city, which awaits future development and ornamentation.

Buildings and Improvements.—The Kaw river flows through the city, and this is spanned by one public bridge. The first bridge was built in 1858 by private enterprise, but was washed away a few years later. In 1870 a second private bridge was built, and was purchased the next year for $100,000, half by the county and half by the city. This allowed a liberal margin above cost to the builders. In 1896 this bridge was replaced by a beautiful Melan arch bridge. This bridge is 540 feet long, and is built of five concrete arches, reenforced with iron. It has a paved roadway and paved sidewalks, 40 feet wide in all. This bridge cost $150,000 and was paid for by the county. But since the city pays approximately two-thirds of the taxes of the county, this was considered a just apportionment.

For the administrative officers, the city first rented isolated office buildings, paying as high as $1,500 a year rental. In 1879 a city hall was completed at a cost of $38,000. Rooms in this not needed by the city were rented for $2,360 a year, thus making a return to the city of 6 per cent. on the investment. In 1900 a city hall and auditorium was completed at a cost of $82,832. Under one roof this building provides suitable offices for the city officials, a council chamber, headquarters for the fire department, and an auditorium capable of seating four thousand five hundred people.

The city has also constructed and maintains three other fire stations, police station and city prison, electric light station, "pest" house, material yards, etc. Annual or monthly appriations are made for maintenance. To meet the extraordinary expenses of construction of all the larger buildings, bonds

were issued.   The city has expended $283,000 for the construc-
tion of the various city buildings.

Administrative Salaries.—There are certain city officers, not
identified with any specialized department, who administer the
affairs of the city as a whole.   Their number and functions
vary with the growth of the city.   At the present time (1904)
the city is making an annual outlay for these administrative
salaries as follows:

Mayor	$1,500
Clerk	1,350
Deputy clerk	600
Attorney	1,200
Treasurer	1,200
Engineer	1,200
Commissioner of elections	1,200
License collector	600
Assessor, $3 per day	
12 councilmen, each	200
City physician	600
Food inspector	800

The following officers have functions readily identified with
differentiated departments:

Superintendent of public schools	$2,500
Police judge	750
Chief of police	1,000
Police matron	600
Street commissioner	1,020
Supt., electric light	1,200
Fire marshal	1,500

Interest.—The city is a heavy borrower of money, and hence
the annual payment of interest is an important item of the
budget.   This amounts to approximately $20,000 on the bonded
debt of the city at large, and $20,000 on the special improvement
bonds, as will be shown in a subsequent paragraph.

Judgments.—Claims of various kinds against the city are
allowed each year, often forming an important item of outlay
for the year.   During the eleven years from 1892 to 1902 the
city expended $74,777 in this manner.

Subsidies and Bonuses.—Topeka, like other Kansas cities, has
favored the policy of subsidizing various business enterprises.
In 1872, $100,000 was given to the Santa Fé railroad company
for the location of the shops and general offices at Topeka.   In

1873, $74,000 was voted to the Kansas Midland railroad in 8 per cent. 20-year bonds. These bonds were refunded when due for twenty years at five per cent. So the city engages to pay the principal, $74,000, and interest $192,400, a total of $266,400. This is rather a liberal way of donating $74,000 to the railroad. In 1901 the Santa Fé was voted further aid in the sum of $59,-000, to enlarge the car shops in the city. In 1886 the city donated $12,000 for the purpose of prospecting for coal. No coal was discovered. The city and county, in 1875, paid $12,000 (half each) for grounds for a state insane asylum, which was accordingly located by the state on this free site.

About the time the Santa Fé shops were built in Topeka, a Cleveland (Ohio) bridge company was interested in establishing a bridge works at Iola, Kansas. They transferred the shops to Topeka upon a vote by the city to give a subsidy of $100,000. The constitutionalty of such public aid to a private industry was seriously doubted, at the time. The Iola bonds were tested by the Supreme Court of the United States and pronounced void.[8] Topeka promptly repudiated her issue; the bridge company failed, and the Santa Fé acquired the plant which had been erected. While this case was pending in 1873, a project was brought forward for founding a steel rail rolling mill in Topeka. $150,000 was voted, and the shops were erected. In 1874 a steel rail was actually produced.

The court decision on the bridge bonds settled the fate of these new bonds. The city recovered them in 1874 and destroyed them. It is not clear yet just what the difference is between a *private* and a *public* enterprise. Hence some subsidies are held constitutional, others unconstitutional.

INCOME

We may classify the city's income as follows:
Gifts,
Interest on deposits,
Rents on city property,
Fines and penalties,

---

[8] *20 Wall.*, 655; *20 Wall.*, 668.

Fees and licenses,

Special assessment,

Taxation.

The relative importance of each source is readily seen from this table showing income for fiscal year ending March 31, 1904.

Interest on deposits	$1,920 45
Rent of auditorium	683 92
Fines and penalties	5,067 26
Fees and licenses	6,114 30
Special assessments	70,933 75
Taxes	383,266 00
Total	$467,985 68

Gifts.—For ornamentation, utility and other purposes, Topeka has received various gifts from her citizens. A $44,000 city library building is the most conspicuous of these. A benevolent clergyman donated a drinking fountain and also provided funds for the erection of a women's apartment to the city prison.

Interest on deposits.—The city funds, including sinking funds are kept on deposit with banks and yield the city 2 per cent. interest.

Rents on city property.—The city owns a large auditorium which is under the administration of a committee on public buildings. This committee leases the auditorium at rates varying from $5 to $75 a day, according to the nature of the entertainment given. Eight classes are described in the city ordinance.[9] In the case of national or state gatherings attracting at least five hundred people to the city, the use of the hall is granted free. The small annual income from this source is about sufficient to keep the auditorium in good repair.

The city also owns scales for weighing wagon-loads of hay, etc., for the farmers, and these scales now afford $700 to $800 a year income to the city.

Fines and Penalties.—An income of some $5,000 a year is now derived from this source. This is turned into the general revenue fund of the city, but it is not large enough to cover the pay-roll of the city police force.

---

[9] Ordinance. No. 2492. Published May 6, 1904.

Fees and Licenses.—According to the charter, Topeka's mayor and council may levy a license tax upon "any and all callings, trades, professions, and occupations conducted, pursued, carried on or operated within the limits" of the city.[10] This is rather a blanket provision, for local sentiment has always been in favor of a wide use of licenses. In 1887, for instance, we find an ordinance passed, providing for forty-six licenses and covering all occupations of the city, from the merchant, the doctor and dentist to the peddler and corn doctor.[11] Some of these license were as follows:

Attorneys at law......................................	$10 a year
Corn doctors	$2 a day
Dentists	$10 a year
Doctors	$10 a year
Merchants	$20 a year
Book Agent	$1 a day
Lumber Dealer	$50 a year
Circus	$300 a day

Twelve corporations were listed for annual license taxes as follows:

American District Telegraph..............................	$25
Electric Light Company	$100
Express Company	$100
Gas Company	$100
Insurance Company	$25
Oil Tank Company ....;	$100
Street Railroad Company..................................	$100
Telegraph Company	$100
Telephone Company	$100
Water Company	$100
Street Paving Company	$100
Railroad Company	$100

A new city ordinance covering the subject went into effect in 1902.[12] This ordinance extended the list to cover fifty-two enumerated occupations, but removed from the list the ordinary, established businesses and professions such as merchants, lawyers,

---

[10] *Laws of Kansas,* 1903, ch. 122.
[11] City Ordinance. No. 767.
[12] Ordinance No. 2384. Published Dec. 24, 1903.

doctors, etc.   Instead of twelve corporations, only six were enumerated, and with the following licenses:

Insurance company.................................... $25 a year
Gas company .... 150 a year
Electric light company............................... 150 a year
Electric light and heating company, for heating........... 75 a year
Telegraph company .... 100 a year
Express company .... 100 a year

Peddlers and solicitors were divided into nine classes with licenses to suit, but with the proviso, ''nothing in this ordinance shall require payment of license tax by persons selling only hay, grain, vegetables, meats and articles of their own raising, or by the residents of the city on articles of their own manufacture.''

The ''dog tax'' is one of the most successful licenses in operation.   A dog officer is chosen by the mayor and council, on a salary of $60 a month, to enforce the ordinance.[13]   Dogs must be registered with the city clerk, the license tax being two dollars a year for male dogs, and seven dollars a year for female dogs.   This brings in to the city from ten hundred to fifteen hundred dollars a year, net revenue, besides tending to eliminate the mongrel breed of dogs.

Special Assessment.—The expense of sewers and street and alley paving is met by special assessment.   This is levied on a ''benefit district,'' that is, on abutting property to the distance of three hundred feet, but in no case does the benefit district extend more than half way to the street or public highway parallel with and next to the public grounds to be improved. The special assessment tax is certified to by the city clerk, and collected by the county treasurer along with the regular taxes. The city sells ''internal improvement'' bonds to cover the cost of the special improvement, and the property owner benefited pays a special assessment tax annually for a series of years— usually ten—sufficient to retire these bonds.   The unusually wide streets in some parts of Topeka have made the burden of paving very heavy as shown in a preceding paragraph.   Areas at street intersections are paved at the city's expense.

---

[13] Ordinance No. 2468.   Published Dec. 23, 1903.

Taxation.—Direct taxation forms by far the most important source of the city's revenue. Methods of assessment and levy have been described before.

The table below is interesting as furnishing a complete exhibition of the city's assessment since 1862, with absolute and relative amounts for realty, personalty, and railroads:

TOTAL ASSESSMENT OF TOPEKA, 1862–1904.
(From manuscript records in county treasurer's office.)

Year.	Realty.	Personalty.	Railroads.	Total.
1904	$8,413,688	$2,309,390	$501,834	$11,224,912
1903	8,299,745	2,317,975	491,457	11,109,177
1902	8,150,325	1,981,670	399,947	10,531,942
1901	7,917,530	1,882,405	374,230	10,174,165
1900	7,699,935	1,768,525	363,035	9,831,495
1899	7,082,335	1,454,240	351,067	8,887,642
1898	7,121,120	1,352,920	381,754	8,855,794
1897	7,850,390	1,354,560	359,934	9,564,884
1896	7,819,955	1,401,295	393,953	9,615,203
1895				
1894	7,563,235	1,611,590	359,737	9,534,563
1893	7,272,700	1,676,900	379,753	9,329,354
1892	7,226,370	1,669,615	314,756	9,210,741
1891	7,758,945	1,987,845	309,561	10,056,351
1890	7,682,460	2,040,945	353,655	10,077,060
1889	6,165,055	2,709,620	354,164	9,228,839
1888	5,839,645	2,544,486	351,648	8,735,779
1887	5,154,719	1,794,481	320,817	7,270,017
1886	4,760,068	1,474,153	312,857	6,547,078
1885	4,402,565	1,251,157	276,201	5,929,923
1884	4,234,235	1,147,299	235,657	5,617,191
1883	3,585,992	970,106	160,219	4,716,317
1882	3,271,804	821,820	109,379	4,203,003
1881	2,677,435	608,230	124,770	3,410,435
1880	2,412,049	489,602	102,988	3,004,639
1879	1,765,205	487,356	85,734	2,338,295
1878	1,667,756	699,069	58,661	2,425,486
1877	1,864,723	668,863	42,371	2,575,957
1876	1,838,242	717,817	40,669	2,596,728
1875	1,692,799	775,914		2,468,713
1874	1,668,719	817,883	R. R.	2,486,602
1873	1,789,342	1,091,752	included in	2,881,094
1872	1,823,504	1,210,544	"Personality"	3,034,048
1871	1,685,596	946,354	prior to 1876.	2,631,950
Township and City.				
1870	632,904	41,076		673,980
1869	701,275	85,651		786,926
1868	311,705	66,584		378,289
	Realty.	**Personalty.**	**Town Lots.**	
1867	366,255	459,120	632,335	1,457,710
1866	346,490	350,524	545,171	1,242,185
1865	237,636	161,710	298,825	698,171
1864	229,676	80,298	290,425	600,399
1863	229,676	63,174	290,785	583,635
1862	170,958	51,702	230,796	453,456

There was formerly a limit to the levy, which was two per cent., but this excluded levies for purposes of schools, waterworks, sewers, special improvements and paving street cross-

,ings. Hence it was a fictitious limit. At present, the levy limit, according to the city charter is,

General revenue .... 6 mills
General improvement .... 6 mills
Interest .... no limit
Water ....4 mills
Judgments ....1 mill

Omitting school levy and special assessment, which are distinct items in municipal bookkeeping, the city clerk's records show the following tax levy:

TOPEKA, TAX LEVY, 1893–1904, RATE IN MILLS

Purpose	1893	1894	1895	1896	1897	1898	1899	1900	1901	1903	1904
General revenue....	6	6	6	6	6	6	6	6	6	6	6
General improvement	5	5	5.5	5	5	5.5	6	6	6	6	6
Interest	2.1	2.1	2.1	2	2	2	2	2	1.5	2	2
Water...............	1.6	1.6	1.6	1.6	1.75	2	2	1	1	1	1.5
Library	.5	.5	.5	.5	.5	.5	.5	.5	.5	.5	.5
Judgment	.5	.5	2.5	2.5	1						
Internal improvement bonds (city's share)........	4.9	4.9	5	4.55	1.65	1.4	1	1	1	1.5	2
Internal imp. interest (city's share).						.4	.5	.5	.5	1	1
Sinking fund					1	1.2	.5				
Parks					1	1.2	.5	... ..	.5	.5	1
Total..........	20.6	20.6	23.2	22.15	18	19	18.5	17	17	18.5	20

The ordinary tax payer of Topeka, that is, one who is free from any special assessment burden, finds himself taxed for the following purposes, and at the following rates:

TAX LEVY FOR ALL PURPOSES IN TOPEKA, SPECIAL ASSESSMENT ALONE OMITTED. RATE IN MILLS.

| Year. | State. | County. | | | | | | City. | | | | |
		General revenue.	R. R. interest, etc.	Poor.	Fund and interest.	Improvements.	Total county and state.	General revenue.	Library.	School.	Total city.	Grand total.
1892.....	3.80	3.50	1.50	......	.20	.....	9.00	19.80	.50	9.80	30.10	39.10
1894.....	3.80	4	1.60	1	.50	.4	11.30	20.10	.50	10.	30.60	41.90
1895.....	4.20	4.	1.50	1	.60	.5	11.80	22.70	.50	10.	33.30	45.
1896.....	3.90	4.	2.20	1	.10	.8	12.	21.65	.50	10.	32.2⅗0	44.15
1897.....	3.70	4.	3.20	1	.20	.9	13.	18.50	.50	10.	29.	42.
1898.....	3.90	4.	3.20	1	.20	.9	13.20	18.50	.50	11.	30.	43.20
1899.....	5.25	4.	2.60	1	.35	.8	14.	18.	.50	16.	34.50	48.50
1900.....	4.90	3.50	2.25	1	.50	.85	13.	16.50	.50	16.	33.	46.
1901.....	5.20	4.	2.40	1	.10	2.8	15.50	16.50	.50	15.50	32.50	48.

A poll tax or road tax, calling on each man for three dollars in money or two days' labor, is still partially enforced. In 1892 this tax yielded $8,513 in cash and the labor of 257 men. In 1893 it yielded $6,949 in cash.

MUNICIPAL DEBT

As the law is interpreted today, there are practically no limitations on the city's debt. The city early had a small floating indebtedness, for in January, 1859, the city council provided for an issue of $500, city scrip.[14] But a bonded debt soon became the rule, for the city's credit was always jealously guarded and kept equal to that of the best private corporations. In 1899 a block of city bonds sold as low as 3¾ per cent. Straight 20-year, 4 per cent. bonds recently sold at a fair premium. At times of a tight money market the city has issued a few bonds, in recent years, at 4½ per cent. and received a very liberal premium. Some special improvement bonds were issued at 5 per cent. and sold for premium enough to make the rate 4¾ per cent. The bonded debt of the city is shown below:

BONDED INDEBTEDNESS OF CITY AT LARGE

Date of bond	Object	Amount	Interest	Due
July 2, 1886	Refund	$14,000	5 pr ct..	July 2, '06
July 20, 1885................	Refund	14,000	6	July 20, '05
July 15, 1890	Fund..	79,000	5	July 15, '10 '
April 20, 1886.......... ...	Coal Pros	12,000	6	April 20, '06
August 10, 1891...........	Refund (R. R. aid.).....	100,000	....	Aug. 10, '11
November 3, 1893	Refund	74,000	5	Nov. 8, '13
September 1, 1895........	Refund	3,500	5	Sept. 1, '15
January 16, 1899..... ...	Refund	13,000	3¾	Jan. 16, '19
January 1, 1900..........	City Hall	60,000	4	Jan. 1, '20
June 1, 1901	R. R. aid (A., T &. S.F.)	59,000	4	June 1, '31
Total	....	$428,500		

[14] Giles, p. 126 ff.

INTERNAL IMPROVEMENT BONDS

	:Streets	Alley	Sewer
Total outstanding April 1, 1898.............	$87,807	$9,229	$44,864
Issued, 1899-1900	127,034	....	43,549
Issued, 1900-1901	88,605	....	....
Issued, 1901-1902	156,702	....	....
Total outstanding April 1, 1902, $386,378.			

The sinking fund is not invested, but is kept on deposit with local banks, where it draws 2 per cent. interest.

MUNICIPAL BUDGET AND ACCOUNTING

The fiscal year begins April 1. Estimates are made by heads of departments, and these estimates go before the city council. Fixed items, such as salaries, are allowed without debate, but responsibility for flexible charges rests with the council and mayor. Appropriations are made for one month.

In accounting, the fund system is used, transfers often being made from one fund to another to meet unforeseen shortages. As yet no logical, and, it may be truthfully added, no intelligible system of bookkeeping has been used. The city treasurer, who is also school treasurer, is the nominal custodian of city funds. He gives a bond of $50,000. He receives all taxes, fees, licenses, etc., giving duplicate receipt, one of which goes to the city clerk. As a matter of fact, the county treasurer has books open for all city taxes, and he in turn pays these over to the city treasurer. The city clerk keeps accounts with the city and county, and exercises the power of audit. The city funds are largely kept on deposit with the city banks furnishing proper security, and 2 per cent. interest is paid to the city. The city's warrants or checks are payable by any bank in the city, or by the city treasurer.

The most pressing need of the city's fiscal system is a clear, comprehensible method of accounting, that shall clearly indicate the exact amount and source of all revenues, the precise expenditures for each separate department (outlay for maintenance and outlay for construction completely differentiated), and some definite allowance for depreciation of city property. This condition is far from being realized at present.

APPENDIX A.

PERCENTAGE OF ASSESSED VALUATION OF EACH CLASS OF PROPERTY, 1861 TO 1900.

Year	Lands	Town lots	Personal	Railroads	Year	Lands	Town lots	Personal	Railroads
1861	49.90	50.10	....	......	1881	53.47	13.17	20.17	13.19
1862	72.43	16.46	11.11	....	1882	52.38	14.08	20.50	13.04
1863	73.05	13.93	13.02	....	1883	49.50	13.61	23.55	13.34
1864	62.89	17.27	20.00	....	1884	49.50	14.68	23.80	12.02
1865	50.76	19.87	29.37	....	1885	49.50	15.49	22.78	12.23
1866	54.08	19.38	26 54	....	1886	51.81	16.95	20.00	11.24
1867	51.03	21.48	27.49	... .	1887	49.02	18.21	19.57	13.20
1868	51.87	18.01	30.12	....	1888	48.07	21.00	15.90	15.03
1869	51.54	18.15	30.31	....	1889	48.08	21.18	14.74	16.00
1870	53.47	17.78	28.75	....	1890	48.50	20.86	14.00	16.64
1871	54.30	16.40	29.30	....	1891	49.75	21.69	13.74	14.82
1872	58.13	16.03	25.84	....	1892	51.28	19.57	13.79	15.36
1873	57.90	16.57	17.79	7.85	1893	50.01	18.80	13.36	17.83
1874	56.30	14.93	17.24	11.42	1894	51.80	18.43	12.14	17.63
1875	59.20	14.74	15.97	11.00	1895	52.63	18.80	10.62	17.95
1876	57.12	13.49	17.36	12.10	1896	51.81	18.38	11.21	18.60
1877	57.14	13.46	18.00	11.40	1897	51.82	18.20	11.73	18.25
1878	53.13	12.14	18.58	11.25	1898	50.59	17.57	13.92	17.92
1879	57.47	12.30	19.00	11.23	1899	50.11	17.12	14.99	17.78
1880	54.41	12.98	19.84	12.77	1900	48.06	17.95	16.46	17.53

NOTE.—In 1861 personal property is included in town lots. Up to 1873 railroads are included in personal property.

APPENDIX Aa.

ASSESSED VALUATIONS OF REAL AND PERSONAL PROPERTY OTHER STATES.[1]

(Percentage of Each Class of Property.)

Year	Real Estate		Personal Property	
	New York	Illinois	New York	Illinois
	Per cent	Per cent	Per cent	Per cent
1867	74.61	....	25.39	....
1868	77.64	....	22.36	....
1869	76.43	....	23.57	....
1870	77.47	....	22.53	....
1871	75.82	....	24.18	....
1872	78.60	....	21.40	....
1873	79.13	70.89	20.87	29.11
1874	79.78	74.22	20.22	25.78
1875	81.11	75.34	18.89	24.66
1876	86.96	77.25	13.04	22.75
1877	87.94	78.81	12.60	21.19
1878	87.44	79.54	12.06	20.46
1879	86.75	79.53	13.25	20.47
1880	87.78	77.85	12.22	22.15
1881	85.63	78.02	14.37	21.98
1882	87.40	77.99	12.60	22.01
1883	89.04	77.94	10.96	22.06
1884	90.06	78.51	9.94	21.49
1885	89.66	79.01	10.31	20.99
1886	89.93	79.77	10.07	20.23
1887	90.00	79.30	10.00	20.70
1888	90.00	79.82	10.00	20.18
1889	90.07	78.19	9.93	21.81
1890	89.54	78.46	10.46	21.54
1891	89.89	79.98	10.11	20.02
1892	89.70	79.76	10.30	20.24
1893	88.06	80.87	11.94	19.13
1894	87.23	78.78	12.77	21.22
1895	88.79	79.86	11.21	20.14
1896	89.48	80.18	10.52	19.82
1897	89.67	80.96	10.33	19.04
1898	88.80	80.42	11.20	19.58
1899	86.95	78.55	13.05	21.45
1900	88.10	....	11.90	....
1901	88.30	....	11.70	....
1902	89.83	....	10.17	....

[1] Sources of table:
For New York—Report of State Board of Tax Com., 1902, p. 42.
For Illinois—Auditors' Reports, 1883, table 33; 1890, table 27; 1900, table 29.

APPENDIX B

RECEIPTS AND EXPENDITURES FOR COMMON SCHOOLS.

From Biennial Reports of State Superintendent of Public Instruction.

Year	Balance on hand	School tax	School fund	Bonds and other sources	Total receipts	Total expenditures	Per capita exp'use
1899	$550,986 90	$3,608,482 35	$400,352 79	$409,249 56	$4,969,071 60	$4,360,472 94	$3 07
1900	600,168 32	3,897,873 10	421,133 94	358,526 75	5,277.702 11	4,622,363 76	3 14
1901	655,338 89	3,850,557 15	387,561 41	345,613 36	5,238,970 81	4,566,209 53	3 04

APPENDIX C.

MORTGAGE STATISTICS FOR 1890 (11TH U. S. CENSUS).

State	Total number	Total Amount	On Acres		On Lots	
			Number	Amount	Number	Amount
Kansas......	298,884	$243,146,826	203,306	$174,720,071	95,578	$68,426,755
Nebraska ...	155,377	132,902,322	107,105	90,506.968	48,202	42,395,354
Missouri'. ..	192,028	214,609,772	103,161	101,718,625	88,867	112,891,147
Colorado....	54,600	85,058,793	20,484	30,195,056	34,116	54,863,737

FARM MORTGAGES IN KANSAS COMPARED WITH UNITED STATES AS A WHOLE.

(Per Cent of Acres Incumbered Each Year, 1886 to 1890.)

	1886	1887	1888	1889	1890
	Per cent.	Per cent.	Per cent.	Per cent.	Per cent.
Kansas ......,.............	60.38	68.92	72.70	70.29	60.32
United States...............	29.28	29.22	29.16	29.14	28.86

APPENDIX D.

RECEIPTS AND DISBURSEMENTS, 1861–1902.

(From State Treasurers' Reports.)

Year	Receipts including transfers.	Disbursements including transfers.	Balances	Year	Receipts including transfers	Disbursements including transfers.	Balances
1861	$46,735	$46,735	......	1882	$2,033,054	$1,817,644	$644,324
1862	47,662	47,662	......	1883	1,852,271	1,658,163	838,432
1863	179,753	168,521	$11,232	1884	2,402,944	2,486,864	754,512
1864	262,534	231,637	42,129	1885	2,394,715	2,403,877	745,350
1865	180,920	196,971	26,079	1886	3,026,496	3,187,573	584,273
1866	371,771	368,919	28,931	1887	2,779,606	2,932,501	431.878
1867	510,347	503,666	35,612	1888	3,048,010	3,154,506	324,882
1868	735,715	711,218	60,109	1889	3,009,356	2,995,493	338,746
1869	1,120,803	1,132,821	48,091	1890	3,109,837	2,733,444	715,138
1870	1,359,653	1,347,397	60,347	1891	3,042,986	5,296,622	461,502
1871	1,047,398	964,228	143,517	1892	2,702,769	2,437,109	727,163
1872	1,295,355	1,298,228	140,645	1893	2,790,571	2,622,193	895,540
1873	1,308,821	1,246,180	203,286	1894	2,445,796	2,499,010	842,326
1874	1,011,068	991,473	222,880	1895	2,578,324	2,710,235	710,415
1875	956,738	1,055,874	123,745	1896	2,451,252	2,560.138	604,529
1876	1,222,088	1,099,716	246,117	1897	2,432,624	2,674,127	463,026
1877	629,229	496,299	379,047	1898	2,721,209	2,672,083	412,152
1878	1,263,182	1,329,418	312,811	1899	2,939,385	2,853,087	498,450
1879	1,344,779	1,250,199	407,391	1900	3,920,907	3,908,646	510,711
1880	1,610,674	1,573,367	444,698	1901	3,693,935	3,627,021	577,626
1881	1,691,340	1,677,124	458,914	1902	3,595,350	3,545,609	627,367

APPENDIX Da.

TOTAL ASSESSED VALUATIONS, AMOUNT OF STATE TAX LEVY AND RATE IN MILLS.

(From State Treasurers' Reports).

Year	Assessed valuation	Levy	Rate	Year	Assessed valuation	Levy	Rate
1861.....	$24,737,563	$74,234	4	1884....	237,020,391	1,066,592	$4\frac{1}{2}$
1862.....	19,285,749	115,737	8	1885....	248,846,811	1,032,714	$4\frac{3}{20}$
1863.....	25,460,499	152,763	7	1886....	277,113,323	1,136,134	$4\frac{1}{10}$
1864.....	30,502,791	182,585	7	1887....	310,871,447	1,274,573	$4\frac{1}{10}$
1865.....	36,120,945	216,757	7	1888....	353,248,333	1,448,318	$4\frac{1}{10}$
1866.....	50,439,645	252,201	6	1889....	360,815,073	1,515,423	$4\frac{2}{10}$
1867.....	56,276,360	281,382	6	1890....	348,459,944	1,480,955	$4\frac{1}{4}$
1868.....	66,949,950	435,408	$6\frac{1}{2}$	1891....	342,632,407	1,353,398	$3\frac{12}{20}$
1869....	76,383,697	763,837	10	1892....	342,682,846	1,336,371	$3\frac{9}{10}$
1870.....	92,528,100	809,621	$8\frac{3}{4}$	1893....	356,621,818	1,358,060	$3\frac{8}{10}$
1871.....	108,753,575	652,521	6	1894....	337,501,722	1,316,258	$3\frac{9}{10}$
1872.....	127,690,937	1,085,373	$8\frac{1}{2}$	1895....	329,939,031	1,402,240	$4\frac{1}{4}$
1873.....	125,684,177	754,105	6	1896....	321,216,938	1,365,171	$4\frac{1}{4}$
1874.....	128,906,520	773,439	6	1897....	325,370,232	1,333,954	$4\frac{1}{10}$
1875.....	121,544,344	729,266	6	1898....	325,889,747	1,346,126	$4\frac{1}{10}$
1876.....	133,832,316	736,078	$5\frac{1}{2}$	1899....	327,165,530	1,799,409	$5\frac{1}{2}$
1877.....	137,480,530	756,138	$5\frac{1}{2}$	1900....	328,729,008	1,807,898	$5\frac{1}{2}$
1878.....	138,698,811	762,843	$5\frac{1}{2}$	1901....	363,156,045	1,997,304	$5\frac{1}{2}$
1879.....	144,930,280	942,046	$5\frac{1}{2}$	1902....	363,163,630	1,997,354	$5\frac{1}{2}$
1880.....	160,570,761	883,139	$5\frac{1}{2}$				
1881.....	170,813,373	854,066	5				
1882.....	186,128,139	837,576	$4\frac{1}{2}$				
1883....	203,184,489	873,693	$4\frac{3}{10}$				

NOTE.—The assessed valuation is about one-fifth of actual value at the present time

APPENDIX E.

PER CAPITA NET DEBT, MUNICIPAL, STATE, AND UNITED STATES.

Year.	Municipal	State	United States
1873...............................	$22 69	$2.01	$50 52
1874...............................	22 84	2.07	49.17
1875...............................	....	2.18	47.53
1876...............................	....	1.71	45.66
1877...............................	....	1.66	43.56
1878...............................	19 30	1.55	42.01
1879...............................	....	1.28	40.87
1880...............................	14 05	1.07	38.27
1881...............................	....	1.03	35.46
1882...............................	13 57	.99	31.91
1883...............................	....	.82	28.66
1884...............................	14 05	.65	26.20
1885...............................	....	.48	24.50
1886...............................	12 42	.59	22.34
1887...............................	....	.52	20.03
1888...............................	20 98	.55	17.72
1889...............................	....	.55	15.92
1890...............................	25 57	.56	14.22
1891...............................	....	.57	13.34
1892...............................	26 76	.57	12.93
1893...............................	....	.58	12.64
1894...............................	27 36	.59	13.30
1895...............................	....	.57	13.08
1896...............................	35 63	.57	13.60
1897...............................	....	.46	13.78
1898...............................	23 21	.45	14.08
1899...............................	....	.48	15.55
1900...............................	22 03	.47	14.52
1901...............................	....	.42	13.45
1902...............................	21 31	.41	12.27

APPENDIX F

MUNICIPAL DEBTS, THEIR GROWTH AND TOTAL AMOUNT.

Year	Railroad aid bonds	Refunding bonds	All bonds issued	Total out-standing debt (net)
1874............................	$358,500	....	$761,610	$12,677,750
1875............................	39,600	....	169,038	....
1876............................	61,900	$120,000	385,600	....
1877–'8........................	646,000	72,867	772,717	13,473,198
1879–'80.......................	1,067,540	....	2,053,672	13,998,604
1881–'2........................	589,485	1,579,800	2,248,125	14,472,019
1883–'4........................	239,500	1,339,234	1,690,732	15,595,126
1885–'6........................	961,000	1,593,529	3,172,390	17,473,347
1887–'8........................	8,544,551	2,378,750	13,338,062	30,733,935
1889–'90.......................	804,250	3,419,030	7,566,689	36,491,660
1891–'2........................	315,000	1,154,240	3,271,831	37,075,740
1893–'4........................	56,500	299,661	1,501,028	36,805.599
1895–'6........................	....	712,900	1,719,677	34,604,246
1897–'8........................	200,000	1,074,000	2,104,552	32,276,339
1899–1900......................	31,500	4,509,140	6,401,333	32,398,799
1901–'2........................	59,000	2,396,602	2,724,100	32,614,909

APPENDIX G.

RAILROAD MILEAGE AND SUBSIDY TABLE.

Year.	Mileage	Increase	Subsidy
1865	55	....	$750,000 00
1866	300	245	450,000 00
1867	540	240	100,000 00
1868	600	60	368,000 00
1869	900	300	1,109,000 00
1870	1,469	569	1,189,000 00
1871	1,770	301	830,000 00
1872	2,039	269	950,000 00
1873	2,063	24	249,000 00
1874	1,839	(224)	358,500 00
1875	2,000	161	39,600 00
1876	2,129	129	61,900 00
1877	2,199	70	646,000 00
1878	2,302	103	
1879	2,444	142	1,067,540 00
1880	3,478	1,034	
1881	3,701	223	589,485 00
1882	3,786	85	
1883	3,870	84	239,500 00
1884	4,020	150	
1885	4,181	161	961,000 00
1886	4,522	341	
1887	6,212	1,690	8,544,550 50
1888	8,312	2,100	
1889	8,721	409	804,250 00
1890	8,763	43	
1891	8,853	90	315,000 00
1892	8,845	(8)	
1893	8,840	(5)	56,500 00
1894	8,832	(8)	
1895	8,829	(3)	0
1896	8,829	0	
1897	8,802	(27)	200,000 09
1898	8,759	(43)	
1899	8,690	(69)	31,500 00
1900	8,717	27	
1901	8,710	(7)	59,000 00
1902	8,754	44	

NOTE.—Numbers in the "increase" column, enclosed in parenthesis indicate a *decrease.*

This table is compiled from the reports of the Board of Railroad Commissioners and of the state auditors.

APPENDIX H.

BANKING: DEPOSITS, RESERVE, ETC.

ALL STATE AND PRIVATE BANKS, 1891–1902

Date of Call	No. of banks.	Total deposits	Legal reserve	Reserve per cent
Oct., 1891......................	414	$15,773,439	$5,477,272	34.09
Jan., 1892.........	439	17,377,978	6,703,668	38.60
June, 1892......................	444	18,445,945	7,341,835	39.80
Jan., 1893..	445	21,139,913	7,449,205	35.24
June, 1893......................	434	19,219,526	6,803,618	35.40
Jan., 1894......................	414	15,427,494	6,194,706	40.15
July, 1894......................	410	16,755,870	5,424,289	44.30
Jan., 1895......................	405	17,112,465	6,575,501	38.42
July, 1895......................	408	16,587,435	6,257,294	37.54
Feb., 1896......................	396	15,526,832	6,023,529	38.80
Sept.,1896......................	392	15,220,107	6,439,657	42.31
Mar., 1897......................	381	15,975,502	6,656,846	41.67
Oct., 1897......................	383	22,004,874	11,072,746	50.32
April, 1898......................	365	22,318,165	10,466,694	46.89
Oct., 1898	366	22,992,900	10,463,441	45.50
Mar., 1899......................	364	23,041,694	10,174,655	44.15
Sept., 1899......................	383	25,956,271	12,074,189	46.51
Feb., 1900......................	387	27,125,275	11,274,840	41.56
Sept., 1900......................	388	31,626,335	16,285,287	51.49
Feb., 1901.............	395	33,760,873	16,057,234	47.56
Sept., 1901..............	422	43,000,004	22,879,490	53.20
Mar., 1902	437	39,830,429	17,060,652	42.83
Sept., 1902......................	462	40,059,291	17,008,196	42.45

APPENDIX I.

VALUE OF STATE PROPERTY, 1902.

(Estimates made by Auditor and Officers in Charge.

Osawatomie Hospital	$800,300
Topeka Hospital	791,100
Parsons Hospital	118,000
Industrial School for Boys......................................	186,050
Industrial School for Girls......................................	115,500
School for Feebleminded..	158,900
Soldiers' Orphans Home..	183,000
School for the Blind..	156,250
School for the Deaf and Dumb..................................	272,965
State University	1,225,000
Agricultural College	1,083,090
Agricultural College Experiment Station.......:.................	74,080
State Normal	570,000
Western Branch Normal..	89,308
Industrial School, Quindaro....................................	21,500
Penitentiary	1,594,500
Industrial Reformatory	510,545
State Soldiers' Home	108,000

Mother Bickerdyke Home..	17,250
Forestry Stations	5,415
Silk Stations	2,500
Executive Residence	35,000
Capitol heating and lighting plant.............................	50,000
Capitol	3,000,000

NOTE:—This includes 1,250 acres of land; $293,375 of libraries; $209,730 of museums; $901,180 of endowments (schools); $38,450 of live stock.

APPENDIX J.

SALARIES OF STATE OFFICERS.

Governor $3,000
Secretary of State	2,500
Auditor	2,500
Treasurer	2,500
Attorney General	2,500
Superintendent of Public Instruction...........................	2,000
Justices of Supreme Court (3), each...........................	3,000
Judges of Appellate Court (6), each...........................	2,500
Judges of District Court (29), each...........................	2,500
Railroad Commissioners (3), each	2,500
Bank Commissioner	2,500
State Architect	2,500
Superintendent of Insurance...................................	2,000
Secretary of Board of Agriculture..............................	2,000
Adjutant General	1,000
Commissioner of Labor Statistics..............................	1,500

BIBLIOGRAPHY

I. PRIMARY SOURCES.

    1. KANSAS DOCUMENTS.

        A. Regular reports, now issued annually or biennially, Topeka, Kansas.

        Auditor (biennial),

        Treasurer (biennial),

        Governor ('Governors' messages; biennial),

        Secretary of State (biennial),

        Attorney-General (biennial),

        Superintendent of Public Instruction (biennial),

        Board of Railroad Commissioners (annual),

        Bank Commissioner (biennial),

        Superintendent of Insurance (biennial),

        Secretary of Board of Agriculture (biennial),

        Adjutant-General (biennial),

        Commissioner of Labor and Industry (biennial).

The auditor's reports show in detail all sources of state revenue, as well as all objects of state outlay. They show also a complete registry of the bonded debts of the state and the munipalities. They are the chief source employed in the foregoing history.

        B. Special reports.

            (1) Sugar industry in Kansas for the year 1890. Report of the state sugar inspector. Topeka, 1891.

            (2) Report of the Joint Legislative Committee, appointed to investigate the affairs and offices of the auditor and treasurer. Topeka, 1870.

(3) Assessment of railroad property in Kan-
.sas, 1879. Topeka, 1879.

(4) Report of the State Auditor, made upon
a request from the Ways and Means
Committee of the Senate and House of
Representatives for information concerning amounts due counties for
maintenance of destitute insane persons, and amounts due the state from
the various counties for back taxes.
Topeka, 1899.

(5) Kansas State Tax Commission Report.
Topeka, 1901.

(6) Proceedings of the Court of Impeachment for the trial of J. E. Hayes,
Treasurer of State. Topeka, 1874.

C. Journals of the Council and House of Representatives.

Kansas Territory, 1855 to 1861.

Journal of the Senate and House of Representatives of Kansas, 1861 and following. Now issued biennially, and also
after each special session of the legislature.

These contain rules and joint rules pertaining
to committees and general budgetary legislation, special reports of legislative committees
bearing on financial matters, and the title and
history of every bill introduced. Since comparatively few bills ever become laws, this
source (aside from its committee reports) is
chiefly important in showing the tendency of
legislation at any one period.

D. Laws of Kansas Territory, 1855 to 1861.

Laws of Kansas, 1861 and following.

This includes the Session Laws, and also the
General Statutes of 1868.
General Statutes of 1889.
General Statutes of 1901.

This source reveals all the tax legislation ever
enacted in Kansas. The General Statutes
also contain, for convenient reference, the
treaty ceding Louisiana to the United States,
the treaty between France and Spain, the
Organic Act, the Constitution of Kansas (including Ordinance, Schedule, and Resolutions), the act of admission (congress), and
the act of admission (Kansas legislature).

E. Kansas Supreme Court Reports.

Reports of decisions are here given, touching
upon the meaning of the various financial
laws whose constitutionality was called in
question.

F. Kansas State Historical Society collections.

This is a collection of miscellaneous source material pertaining especially to the territorial
and early state period.

2. CONGRESSIONAL DOCUMENTS.

A. Report of the Special Committee on the Troubles
in Kansas. House of Representatives, 34 Congress, 1 session. Number 200. Washington,
1856.

B. Blackmar, F. W., Higher Education in Kansas,
Bulletin number 27 in Government Series of
"Contributions to American Educational His-
tory." Washington, 1900.

3. DOCUMENTS ON FINANCIAL HISTORY OF TOPEKA.

A. In manuscript only.—Official reports of city
clerk and treasurer; council journal; assessment rolls (in office of County Treasurer).

B. Published.—Revised Ordinances of City of To-
peka (Topeka, 1888); Laws of Kansas, 1903,
Chapter 122; Report of City Engineer to the
Mayor and City Council, January 1, 1903;
Report of Superintendent of City Electric
Light Department, (Leaflet), 1903.

II. SECONDARY SOURCES.

1. Andreas, A. T., History of the State of Kansas. Chi-
cago, 1883.

A good source on local history, especially.

2. Benton, E. J., Taxation in Kansas.   In Johns Hopkins
University Studies. Vol. 18, pp. 115–176.   Balti-
more, 1900.

A brief but suggestive analytical history of Kansas
taxation.

3. Blackmar, F. W., Life of Charles Robinson.   Topeka,
1902.

Taxation in Kansas.   In the Kansas University Quart-
erly.   Lawrence, 1897.

A short description of the tax system.

4. Canfield, J. H., Taxation (Economic Tract, Kans. His.
Soc. Collections).   New York, 1883.

5. Daniels, ——, Problems in Taxation.   Topeka, 1894.

6. Dennis, E. W., (Attorney of K. P. Ry.), Memoranda
respecting assessment of Railways.   Topeka, 1872.

7. Giles, ——, Review of the Tax System of Kansas. Topeka, 1872.

Thirty years in Topeka.   Topeka, 1886.

8. Hazelrigg, Clara H., A New History of Kansas.   Topeka, 1895.

"A book dedicated to the teaching of patriotism."

9. Hodder, Frank H., Government of the People of Kansas.   Philadelphia, 1895.

A concise exposition of the civil government of Kansas.

10. Holloway, John N., History of Kansas from the first
Exploration of the Mississippi Valley to the admission into the Union.   Lafayette, Ind., 1868.

A good narrative, critically prepared from primary sources.

11. Kansas Miscellaneous Pamphlets.

A collection in the Wisconsin State Historical Society Library.

12. Prentis, Noble L., A History of Kansas. Winfield, Kans., 1899.

13. Prouty, S. S., Topeka Constitutional Scrip, etc., Topeka, 1887.

14. Spring, L. W., Kansas. (American Commonwealth Series.) Boston, 1885.

15. Taylor ——, Tax Laws and Decisions. Topeka, 1884.

16. Waters, A. W., Assessor's Manual, containing all the laws pertaining to valuation and assessment. Topeka, 1890.

17. Wilder, D. W., Annals of Kansas. Topeka, 1875.

An excellent encyclopaedia of facts.

18. Purdue, Rosa M., Genesis of (Kansas) Constitution. In Kansas Historical Collections, Wis. State His. Soc., Vol. 7, pp. 130 seq. Topeka, 1902.

III. OTHER WORKS WHICH ARE CITED.

1. Ely, R. T., Outlines of Economics.

2. Reports of State Tax Commissions of Michigan, Texas, New York and Illinois.

3. United states:

Census reports,

Statistical Abstracts,

Statutes at Large.

Supreme Court Reports.

4. New York Commercial and Financial Chronicle.

5. Leavenworth (Kansas) Journal, Aug. 26, 1858.

6. Herald of Freedom (Lawrence, Kans.), June 20, 1857.

7. Topeka State Journal (Topeka, Kans.), Sept. 6, 1904.

INDEX

1909

BULLETIN OF THE UNIVERSITY OF WISCONSIN

NO. 248

ECONOMICS AND POLITICAL SCIENCE SERIES. Vol. 5. No. 2. pp. 179-294.

THE LABOR ARGUMENT IN THE AMERICAN PROTECTIVE TARIFF DISUSSION

BY

GEORGE BENJAMIN MANOLD

Associate Director St. Louis School of Philanthropy

SUBMITTED FOR THE DEGREE OF DOCOR OF PHILOSOPHY

UNIVERSITY OF WISCONSIN

1906

...hority of law with the approval of the Regents

d entered as second-class matter at the

...e at Madison, Wisconsin

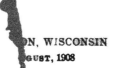

...N, WISCONSIN

...GUST, 1908